Open Source
Fuzzing Tools

Gadi Evron   David Maynor
Noam Rathaus   Charlie Miller
Robert Fly   Yoav Naveh
Aviram Jenik

KEY	SERIAL NUMBER
001	HJIRTCV764
002	PO9873D5FG
003	829KM8NJH2
004	VBPK567AQT
005	CVPLQ6WQ23
006	VBP965T5T5
007	HJJJ863WD3E
008	2987GVTWMK
009	629MP5SDJT
010	IMWQ295T6T

PUBLISHED BY
Syngress Publishing, Inc.
Elsevier, Inc.
30 Corporate Drive
Burlington, MA 01803

Open Source Fuzzing Tools

Printed and bound in the United Kingdom

Transferred to Digital Printing, 2010

ISBN 13: 978-1-59749-195-2

Publisher: Amorette Pedersen   Cover Designer: SPi
Acquisitions Editor: Patrice Rapalus   Page Layout and Art: SPi

For information on rights, translations, and bulk sales, contact Matt Pedersen, Commercial Sales Director and Rights, at Syngress Publishing; email m.pedersen@elsevier.com.

Visit us at

www.syngress.com

Syngress is committed to publishing high-quality books for IT Professionals and delivering those books in media and formats that fit the demands of our customers. We are also committed to extending the utility of the book you purchase via additional materials available from our Web site.

SOLUTIONS WEB SITE

To register your book, visit www.syngress.com/solutions. Once registered, you can access our solutions@syngress.com Web pages. There you may find an assortment of valueadded features such as free e-books related to the topic of this book, URLs of related Web sites, FAQs from the book, corrections, and any updates from the author(s).

ULTIMATE CDs

Our Ultimate CD product line offers our readers budget-conscious compilations of some of our best-selling backlist titles in Adobe PDF form. These CDs are the perfect way to extend your reference library on key topics pertaining to your area of expertise, including Cisco Engineering, Microsoft Windows System Administration, CyberCrime Investigation, Open Source Security, and Firewall Configuration, to name a few.

DOWNLOADABLE E-BOOKS

For readers who can't wait for hard copy, we offer most of our titles in downloadable Adobe PDF form. These e-books are often available weeks before hard copies, and are priced affordably.

SYNGRESS OUTLET

Our outlet store at syngress.com features overstocked, out-of-print, or slightly hurt books at significant savings.

SITE LICENSING

Syngress has a well-established program for site licensing our e-books onto servers in corporations, educational institutions, and large organizations. Contact us at sales@syngress.com for more information.

CUSTOM PUBLISHING

Many organizations welcome the ability to combine parts of multiple Syngress books, as well as their own content, into a single volume for their own internal use. Contact us at sales@syngress.com for more information.

SYNGRESS®

Contributing Authors

Gadi Evron is Security Evangelist for Beyond Security, chief editor of the SecuriTeam portal and recognized globally for his work and leadership in Internet security operations. He is the founder of the Zeroday Emergency Response Team (ZERT), organizes and chairs worldwide conferences, working groups and task forces. He is considered an expert on corporate security and counterespionage, botnets, e-fraud and phishing. Previously, Gadi was CISO at the Israeli government ISP (eGovernment project) and founded the Israeli Government CERT. He has authored two books on information security and is a frequent lecturer.

Noam Rathaus is the co-founder and CTO of Beyond Security. He holds an electrical engineering degree from Ben Gurion University and has been checking the security of computer systems from the age of 13. He is also the editor-in-chief of SecuriTeam.com, one of the largest vulnerability databases and security portals on the Internet.

Robert Fly is a Director of Product Security at Salesforce.com where he works with the great folks there to help deliver a service that the world can trust. At Salesforce.com he heads up the company-wide effort for building security into the development lifecycle. Prior to Salesforce.com Robert worked at Microsoft for about eight years, the last few spent in the Real Time Collaboration Group as a Software Security Lead heading up a team of very talented individuals responsible for ensuring the security of those products.

Aviram Jenik is CEO of Beyond Security and contributor to SecuriTeam.com

David Maynor is CTO of Errata Security, a consulting and product testing cybersecurity company.

Charlie Miller spent five years as a Global Network Exploitation Analyst for the National Security Agency. During this time, he identified weaknesses and vulnerabilities in computer networks and executed numerous successful computer network exploitations against foreign targets. He sought and discovered vulnerabilities against security critical network code, including web servers and web applications. Since then, he has worked as a Senior Security Architect for a financial firm and currently works as a Principal Security Analyst for Independent Security Evaluators, a security firm. He has spoken at the Workshop on the Economics of Information Security, Black Hat, and DEFCON.

He has a B.S. from Truman State University and a Ph.D. from the University of Notre Dame.

Yoav Naveh works as an R&D team leader for McLean based Beyond Security, and one of the chief developers of the beSTORM fuzzing framework. He is a security researcher with 8 years of experience. He holds the rank of Captain in the Israeli Defense Force (ret.) and is a leading authority in the blackbox testing field.

Contents

## Chapter 1

Introduction to Vulnerability Research

Solutions in this chapter:

- Statement of Scope
- Off-by-One Errors
- Programming Language Use Errors
- Integer Overflows
- Bugs and Vulnerabilities
- The Vaunted Buffer Overflow
- Finding Bugs and Vulnerabilities

Statement of Scope

Entire books exist on the topic of computer vulnerabilities and software testing, and it is beyond the scope of this chapter to provide the in-depth knowledge needed to perform software security testing. While fuzzing is one important way to test software for bugs and vulnerabilities, it is important to understand exactly what we are testing for.

This chapter is an introduction to software testing in general, and as such must describe some of the ways software errors come about. While this material is most-likely review, it will at least provide a common starting point for the less-experienced or novice vulnerability researcher.

> **NOTE**
>
> The best laid schemes o' mice an' men gang aft a-gley.
>
> Robert Burns ("To a Mouse")

A computer in and of itself is nothing more than a paperweight, a useless collection of components and circuitry. For the computer to do anything, a *person* must give it a set of instructions the computer can understand. This, in essence, is the art of computer programming.

But it's not that simple. In reality, there is a vast difference between the instructions a computer can act on and the instructions the average person can understand. While it is entirely possible for humans to learn to issue commands in the language of the computer, this process is an extremely inefficient and time-consuming chore. (A statement to which anyone who owned one of the early IMSAI 8080 computers can attest. The earliest IMSAIs accepted only this type of input.)

And, of course, the computer has no corresponding capability to learn a language that humans can understand—it's a one-way street from intelligence to utility. Consequently, "interpreters" (and compilers, which do the same thing as interpreters, but consider the instructions as whole instead of processing them one at a time) were developed that can take English-like phrases and translate them into the specific binary language a computer can act on.

Humans deal very well with abstraction, but computers choke on it. If you tell a three-year-old child to put on his shoes and socks, you will never see him first put on his shoes and then put on his socks—he will instead put his socks on and then his shoes, because he has learned the abstract concept of footwear: your socks go on before your shoes. A computer has no understanding of even the simplest abstraction, and will proceed only as instructed. The greater the degree of abstraction from the minutia of what the computer can understand, the "higher" the language level is. In this regard, not all languages are created equally—some are far more abstract (higher level) than others.

The language with the closest approximation to the language upon which a computer can operate is "assembly language," which is a one-to-one mnemonic representation of machine codes and values upon which the computer can operate. C, and its successor C++, are the most common programming languages in use for commercial application development today, and are far more abstract than assembly is. Other languages are higher level still.

Lost in Translation(s):

"I know that you believe you understand what you think I said, but I'm not sure you realize that what you heard is not what I meant."—Robert McClosky

Translation is the root cause of most programming errors. For example, a project manager translates the requirements from the desired end to the programming team, which members translate to individual programming assignments, which programmers translate the assignment into the proper syntax for the programming language (written by someone else), which programming language interpreter translates that into the corresponding machine code. All those translations are sources of potential programming errors, some of which we will cover in detail next. Keep in mind that the following descriptions of programming errors are not intended to cover all conceivable ways a programming error can lead to problems, but rather to provide a flavor of the topic.

Off-by-One Errors

Although at first blush, it would seem that anyone who cannot count should not program, this error does not exist in the programmer's inability to count, but rather in the way he counts. A particular example of this is the "fencepost" error. How many fence posts are needed to build a fence 25 feet long with posts placed every 5 feet? Well, you *can* compute this by dividing 25 by 5, getting the answer of 5. While this is the correct answer for the number of fence sections you need (S-1 though S-5), it is *not* the correct answer for the number of posts needed. That answer is 6 (P-1 though P-6), as shown in Figure 1.1.

Figure 1.1 Off-by-One Error

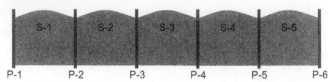

Another error in the off-by-one genre is the use of the wrong comparison operator, such as the "less than" operator (<) instead of the "less than or equal to" operator (<=). For example, an error in a routine printing the numbers 1 to 10 could manifest itself as:

```
#include <stdio.h>
int main(void)
{
int Count = 1;
while (Count <10)
  {
printf("%d",Count);
  ++Count ;
  }
return 0;
}
```

This would instead print the numbers less than 10, in this case the numbers 1 through 9. Changing the "while" statement to:

```
while (Count <=10)
```

corrects this problem.

Off-by-one errors are an example of the programmer translating a concept to the proper algorithm.

Programming Language Use Errors

The function *strcpy* can be used to make a copy of a string in a new location. To do this, it copies each byte from the source address to the destination address, stopping after it copies the special character that signifies the end of the string. Unfortunately, this is all it does. There are no checks that the source or destination are actually valid addresses, no checks that the destination has enough space to hold the source string, and no checks that the locations don't overlap. Provided the programmer uses this function in a safe way, ensuring that the source and destination are valid and that destination can hold all of the source string, no problems will occur. However, if the source string is longer than the space allocated for it, the function will still do exactly what it has been designed to do: copy all the bytes between the start and end of the string to the destination address, including those that are outside of the memory allocated for the second string. While this is probably not what the programmer meant, it is exactly what he asked the computer to do.

The use of *strcpy* has been banned by many programming shops in an effort to minimize the errors its misuse may cause. There is a safer (but not completely safe) function named *strncpy*, which limits the length of the copy to a specified number of bytes. While this sounds better, there are still some "gotchas": the specification only guarantees that it will "null terminate" the string if there is room left at the end. If the programmer doesn't explicitly put the end-of-string null character in, it may be longer than he intended. As an interesting aside, in places where *strcpy* use was banned, programmers sometimes wrote their own functions that duplicated its behavior, right down to its capability to write out of bounds.

Programming language use errors such as this stem from programmers not considering exceptional circumstances.

Integer Overflows

An important data type in any programming language is the integer. Integers can be either signed (with a plus or minus sign) or unsigned.

In a 32-bit operating system, an unsigned integer can range from 0 to +4,294,967,295; the binary representation of those values is shown here:

0	0000 0000 0000 0000 0000 0000 0000 0000
4,294,967,295	1111 1111 1111 1111 1111 1111 1111 1111

Adding 1 to 4,294,967,295 will not give 4,294,967,295, but will instead give 0. To store a larger number would require 33 bits (a 1 followed by 32 0s). The CPU simply stores the lowest 32 bits and makes a note that the number was too big. Multiplying numbers together may also cause an integer overflow. If the programmer assumes that adding or multiplying any two numbers will make a bigger number (which "just makes sense"), and doesn't check for integer overflows, he may introduce a vulnerability. For example, to hold n items that are each m bytes long, the programmer may tell the program to allocate n*m bytes. If $m*n$ is larger than the biggest number that can be represented, less memory will be allocated than intended. This may lead to a buffer overflow.

In the case of a signed integer, which can range from $-2,147,483,648$ to $+2,147,483,647$, it becomes a bit more complicated, because the leftmost bit of the 32-bit is the sign bit—0 for positive and 1 for negative—and the numbers are represented as "two's complements." The binary representation of these values is shown here:

+2,147,483,647	0111 1111 1111 1111 1111 1111 1111 1111
−2,147,483,648	1000 0000 0000 0000 0000 0000 0000 0000

Two's complement representation is the most common means of representing negative numbers, and has many advantages, such as being able to add positive and negative numbers without worrying about the sign bit.

If a programmer assumes that a variable contains only positive integers, but if the integer in question is actually a signed integer, arithmetic operations can cause the overwrite of the leftmost bit and make the results a negative number, possibly leading to exploitable behavior. This scenario is illustrated here:

Unsigned Integer Calculation

2,147,483,647	0111 1111 1111 1111 1111 1111 1111 1111
+1	0000 0000 0000 0000 0000 0000 0000 0001
2,147,483,648	1000 0000 0000 0000 0000 0000 0000 0000

Note the equivalence of the unsigned 2,147,483,648 to the signed −2,147,483,648!

Bugs and Vulnerabilities

Not all programming errors are created equally. Some allow attackers to gain some thing or ability they didn't already have. They may be able to deny other users access to the program by crashing it, or access information they shouldn't be able to. In some cases, they may be able to cause the program to execute any command they tell it. These errors are vulnerabilities.

Other errors, while they may have the same causes, won't give attackers any access they didn't already have.

So, the first task for a vulnerability researcher is to determine if the programming error is merely a bug or if it can lead to exploitation. If a bug can lead to exploitation, either by itself or when used in concert with other bugs, it is indeed a vulnerability.

The Vaunted Buffer Overflow

Most of the vulnerabilities discovered by security researchers are buffer overflows. These overflows are caused by bugs that allow the code to write past the end of a buffer. So, what is a buffer? A buffer is a fixed-size region of memory, set aside for a particular use, usually in the same general location in memory as other values the program uses.

Some vulnerabilities are caused by the application not checking space availability before copying untrusted data into the buffer. Other overflows are more complicated and, while a buffer overflow may be the final effect, the initial cause is usually a bug or series of bugs (e.g., the $m*n$ integer overflows mentioned earlier, off-by-one errors, etc.) somewhere else in the code.

Regardless of the initial cause, without enough space to hold the copied data, the contents of memory outside the buffer will be overwritten. As a result, the next time the program looks at that memory; it sees data from the overflow instead of the original data. If the program tries to use values from that area, it will most likely not see what it expects, the consequences of which can range from a crash of the program to other, more potentially dangerous actions, as shown in Figure 1.2. The address 007e9e0 contains a pointer to the previous stack frame, and 007e9e4 contains the address to execute on return (7e42593f). If a buffer overflow overwrote the contents of 007e9e4 with another address, the program would execute that address when it returned. To understand why this happens, it is first necessary to define a bit more jargon.

Figure 1.2 Part of the Stack in Notepad.exe While Opening a File

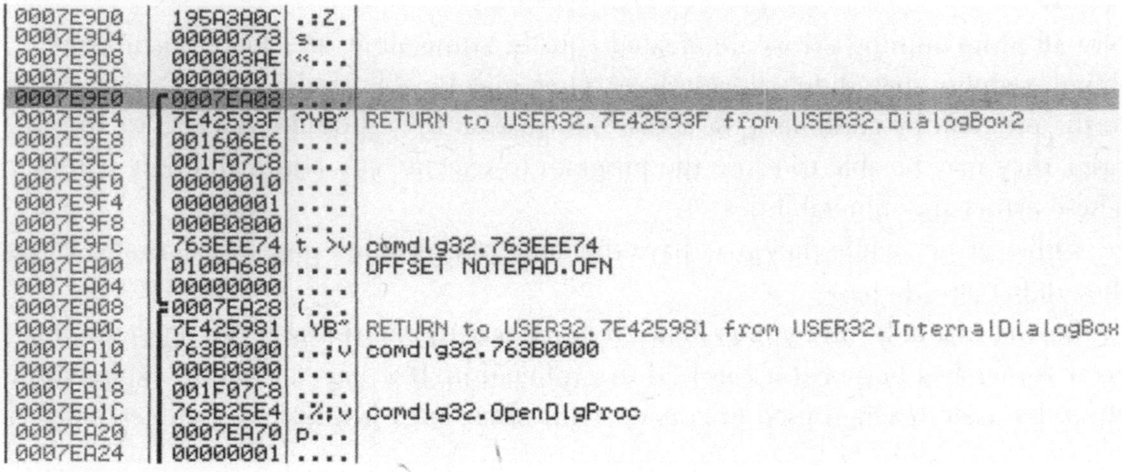

```
0007E9D0    195A3A0C  .:Z.
0007E9D4    00000773  s...
0007E9D8    000003AE  «...
0007E9DC    00000001  ....
0007E9E0   ┌0007EA08  ....
0007E9E4    7E42593F  ?YB"  RETURN to USER32.7E42593F from USER32.DialogBox2
0007E9E8    001606E6  ....
0007E9EC    001F07C8  ....
0007E9F0    00000010  ....
0007E9F4    00000001  ....
0007E9F8    000B0800  ....
0007E9FC    763EEE74  t.>v  comdlg32.763EEE74
0007EA00    0100A680  ....  OFFSET NOTEPAD.OFN
0007EA04    00000000  ....
0007EA08   └0007EA28  (...
0007EA0C    7E425981  .YB"  RETURN to USER32.7E425981 from USER32.InternalDialogBox
0007EA10    763B0000  ..;v  comdlg32.763B0000
0007EA14    000B0800  ....
0007EA18    001F07C8  ....
0007EA1C    763B25E4  .%;v  comdlg32.OpenDlgProc
0007EA20    0007EA70  p...
0007EA24    00000001  ....
```

When a program is running, it requires that the system be in a consistent state. To achieve this, all control structures must contain valid data for the program to work as intended. One such control structure, the "stack," is a section of memory that programs use to record previous activity. When the program calls a function, it must record where it was in the process by storing values on the stack. If attackers can overwrite these values with their own values, when the function ends, it will carry on execution from where they tell it, instead of where it was.

Before proceeding, a confusing subtlety must first be clarified. On mailing lists, sometimes people report a particular crash as a "stack overflow" and suggest that with a little work it could be turned into an exploit, while in reality their issue is (at best) a denial-of-service (DoS) vulnerability. The confusion arises because at least two things can be described as a *stack overflow*—stack-based buffer overflows and unbounded recursion—both of which are capable of crashing a program.

Buffer Overflow on the Stack (aka Stack-based Buffer Overflow)

In this scenario, the program tries to store more data in a buffer located on the stack than it can accommodate. Ultimately, the program tries to use a value that has been overwritten and crashes.

Stack Overflow (aka Unbounded Recursion)

This situation often occurs when a program calls a function that endlessly calls itself (i.e., recursion). Eventually, the "what I was doing" data (found on the stack)

from the previous calls consumes all the available stack space. When the program attempts to call the function again, as there is no space left to store it, it crashes.

While these definitions may sound similar and both cases involve accessing invalid memory, they are very different. A stack-based buffer overflow can allow attackers to execute code on the victim's computer, as it overwrites memory addresses that will be used later, while a "stack overflow" typically results in a DoS, as it tries to write to memory that isn't available.

In any case, the buffer overflow is among the most insidious errors security researchers can find. In fact, the first (known) exploited buffer overflow was in the fingerd service in the Unix systems exploited by the Morris worm. Other notable examples are the Code Red worm that exploiter Microsoft IIS 5.0 and the SQL Slammer worm that exploited MS SQL Server 2000, but researchers have found buffer overflows in practically every program written.

Finding Bugs and Vulnerabilities

Given the multitudinous ways programmers can make mistakes, looking for bugs and vulnerabilities in a piece of software should be an integral part of the development process. Until recently, that has not been the case—a software product is released without any security testing, and it was left up to independent security researchers to find the errors and report them to the vendor for repair. Now, most software faces some kind of security review prior to its release, and many vendors now consider security from the onset of the development project, as is the case with Microsoft's Secure Development Process. But testing the security of a particular product can be an expensive proposition, and vendors must weight that expense with the other cost factors involved in releasing the product to its customers. Because of this, even software developed in an environment stringently cognizant of security risks is most likely released without full testing. Once again, the burden of testing falls upon security researchers. Fortunately, security researchers have a vast array of tools and techniques to locate bugs and vulnerabilities.

Source Code Review

An effective way to find vulnerabilities in software for which the source code is available (such as with open-source software) is manual code review. For example, a researcher may search the source code for instances of the *strcpy* function mentioned earlier, examining each portion of code that uses that function to make sure the function will respect the bounds of the program. While this will show all cases where *strcpy* is improperly used, it will not show cases where a programmer uses a similar technique or function to accomplish the same results.

While this approach has yielded a good many vulnerabilities in the past, its results are predicated on looking for instances of a known language problem or for instances of commonly used statements that are known to exist and cause problems.

Black Box Testing

As the name implies, black box testing does not take into account the actual programming of the application, but rather the input specifications of the program (what data the program is meant to receive) and output specification of the program (what the program is supposed to do with the input data). Black box testing is intended to gauge whether the program complies with the design goals.

From a security perspective, it is important in black box testing to provide the program with input the program normally would not expect, to see how the program deals with this input.

Black box testing can be done manually, or its input and analysis of its output can be automated.

Glass Box Testing

Glass box testing is performed in a similar manner to black box testing, but the testers have a view of the program structure and data flow requirements. With this type of testing, it is easier to make sure the program will function as intended, as it is possible to directly test conditionals in the program flow. With glass box testing, it is possible to craft input that allows every line of code to be executed and tested.

From a security perspective, it is important in glass box testing to provide the program with input the program normally would not expect in order to see how the program deals with this input.

Glass box testing can be done manually or its input can be automated, but the automation is predicated on making sure each of the flows in the program will be exercised.

## Chapter 2

Fuzzing—What's That?

Solutions in this chapter:

- Introduction to Fuzzing
- Milestones in Fuzzing
- Fuzzing Technology
- Second-Generation Fuzzing
- File Fuzzing
- Host-side Monitoring
- Vulnerability Scanners as Fuzzers
- Uses of Fuzzing
- Open Source Fuzzers
- Commercial-Grade Fuzzers
- What Comes Next
- The Software Development Life Cycle

Introduction

In this chapter, we describe in detail what fuzz testing, also known as fuzzing, is and how it works.

The purpose of this chapter is to reach common ground and establish basic terminology for the evolving field of fuzzing, and describe the advances made recently in *Protocol-based Fuzzing* with the introduction of commercial fuzzing products into the market. By the end of this chapter, you will have a good understanding of how fuzzing works, and some steps you can take to implement and use fuzzing.

Fuzzing is often described as a black-box software testing technique. It works by automatically feeding a program multiple input iterations that are specially constructed in an attempt to trigger an internal error indicative of a bug, and potentially crash it.

Such program errors and crashes are indicative of the existence of a security vulnerability, which can later be researched and fixed.

We begin with a short summary of the state of the practice of fuzzing and a quick overview of fuzzing history. We continue with a detailed description of how fuzzing works. We then describe new advances made with fuzzing technology, introduce second-generation fuzzing, and try to assess the usability of fuzzing and what the future holds for this new market.

Fuzzing as a black box testing field, in our opinion, is going to turn into a significant portion of the vulnerabilities and software/application security markets from all ends, prevention to countermeasures.

Fuzzing is not a perfect solution, but when done efficiently it can eliminate many vulnerabilities in the code-space and provide a return-on-investment that far outweighs its implementation costs.

Introduction to Fuzzing

Fuzzing has several dictionary definitions, the most applicable of which is "to become blurred or obscure"; meaning to alter something so it becomes less obvious, or rather confusing. The relation of the term with fuzz testing in computer science is basic at best.

The story of how *fuzzing* got to be the term describing a "black box testing technique" varies depending on who you ask. (Black box testing is testing without prior knowledge or source code. Fuzzing is sometimes referred to as gray box testing, as some information about the internal system design can be used in conjunction with the test). Some say that when Professor Barton Miller wrote fuzz, he named it after the way they used to test electrical lines. Another story is that fuzzing comes from fuzzy logic.

Professor Barton Miller spoke of the history in an e-mail conversation with Gadi Evron: "In the fall of 1989, I was on a dial-up modem to my campus computer. There was a big, Midwest thunderstorm that was causing noise on the phone line (this was before error-correction modems), so it was a race to type a command before a stream of nonsense characters would interfere. I was surprised that these seemingly random characters would occasionally cause Unix utilities to crash. So, as one of my suggested projects in my graduate OS class (CS736), I assigned a project of writing a random character generator and testing as many Unix utility programs as possible. I called this random stream "fuzz," named after the noise on the phone line. It had nothing to do with fuzzy logic or any other field. And I'm not sure why I picked the particular word fuzz."

Fuzzing, fault injection, assumption violating, and other terms were used in the past to describe this technique. What it does is send input to a program (software or hardware) in an attempt to trigger an error indicative of a bug, and potentially a vulnerability (a successful *test case*). (In software testing, test cases pass or fail—rather than succeed—as defined at the offset.)

In this chapter, we use the term *fuzzing* to describe a continuous (automated) brute-force attack of mutated input iterations, attempting to break a program by using the right iteration or combination.

Testing operates under a few assumptions:

- Testing can only prove the presence of bugs, not their absence—Edsger Dijkstra

- Due to Turing completeness, testing may never finish.

- Fuzzing operates under two more specific assumptions regardless of their correctness.

- There are vulnerabilities to be found in the program.

- Given enough input, these vulnerabilities will surface.

This can be a lengthy process; analogies to demonstrate this are drilling into a wall, driving up a hill, and water eroding a stone.

None of these analogies is perfect, as the parameters for them can vary considerably depending on the condition of the wall, road, or stone, and specification of the drill, car, or river.

Fuzzing is better comparable to lock picking, trying all possible keys that may or may not fit, smaller keys, often-used keys, a combination of rods and strings, etc.

Fuzzing is dependent on technological parameters ranging from how well the code was written and how advanced the fuzzer is, to the strength of the CPU running the fuzzer. If the drill from our first analogy was used on the weakest spot in the concrete wall first, results may come quickly.

Wikipedia defines fuzzing as:

"Fuzz testing or fuzzing is a software testing technique. The basic idea is to attach the inputs of a program to a source of random data ("fuzz"). If the program fails (for example, by crashing, or by failing built-in code assertions), then there are defects to correct.

The great advantage of fuzz testing is that the test design is extremely simple, and free of preconceptions about system behavior."

If we are to fine-tune this definition:

Fuzzing is a software testing technique that by providing a program with malformed input, attempts to reach an error indicating a potential vulnerability. Fuzzing does not require previous knowledge about the program tested such as its design or source code, although it can make use of them (black box and gray box testing).

Simplified further, fuzzing is:

Creating malformed input for the program tested and seeing what happens.

This applies to a network service as much as it would to a CPU, a cell phone, program parameters, an API, a Web browser, or a file type.

Many different types of test software can be considered fuzzers by that definition, but not very efficient ones. As an example, stress testing is a form of fuzzing, but an extremely limited and primitive one that measures the stability of the program by emulating a DoS attack.

Any program receiving input can be fuzzed.

Milestones in Fuzzing

Fuzzing has been around for a long time but was commonly referred to as "fault injection" (mostly used in the hardware world).

Fuzzing in the context of the security world was introduced in 1989 by Professor Barton Miller and his students at the University of Wisconsin Madison with the creation of fuzz. They have this to say about it:

"Fuzz testing is a simple technique for feeding random input to applications. While random testing is a time-honored technique, our approach has three characteristics that, when taken together, makes it somewhat different from other approaches.

1. The input is random. We do not use any model of program behavior, application type, or system description. This is sometimes called *black box* testing. In the command-line studies (1990, 1995, and 2006), the random input was simply random ASCII character streams. For our X-Window study (1995), Windows NT study (2000), and Mac OS X study (2006), the random input included cases that had only valid keyboard and mouse events.

2. Our reliability criteria are simple: if the application crashes or hangs, it is considered to fail the test; otherwise, it passes. Note that the application does not have to respond in a sensible manner to the input, and it can even quietly exit.

3. As a result of the first two characteristics, fuzz testing can be automated to a high degree and results can be compared across applications, operating systems, and vendors."

In other words, fuzz was used to send random input to the application until it crashed or hanged.

Skipping a decade ahead, in 2002, Dave Aitel released a paper called "The Advantages of Block-Based Protocol Analysis for Security Testing" along with a fuzzing tool named SPIKE.

What was new about SPIKE's approach was that the random data generated was tied in to regular input the application would expect to see. That in itself wasn't completely new. What was new is that the randomness was tied in to specific parts of the input. Further, SPIKE offered a framework by which new data-set templates could be added to it so that other protocols can be fuzzed.

As an example, a basic protocol request *Data-set* template would look like this:

```
GET /file.name HTTP/1.1
```

The *block-based* approach could tell the fuzzer to send random data at a certain point, such as this block signified by **[ ]**s:

```
GET /[]file.name HTTP/1.1
```

In 2004, two *block-based* fuzzing tools named Peach and smudge (which are very similar to SPIKE) were released. The big advantage of Peach and smudge was that they presented an easy-to-use framework for quick development, adapting them to fuzz anything anyone could set his mind to.

They are both very similar to SPIKE (being *data-set based* and using *block-based fuzzing)*, with two main differences:

- The framework and engine were built more robustly and for easier development.

- They were built in Python (while SPIKE was built in C).

In the past year (2006), second-generation fuzzing was introduced with the appearance of several commercial-grade fuzzers.

If we are to quantify milestones in fuzzing, the main ones are:

- Combining random input generation with application monitoring (fuzz)

- Tying the random input generation with a data-set template (SPIKE)

- Protocol-based fuzzing (beginning of "Second-Generation Fuzzing")

Fuzzing Technology

Fuzzing works in mysterious ways, but there is not much magic to it. Fuzzing can be divided into three main components:

- Fuzzing baseline

- Input generation

- Application monitoring

Input being sent is generated from the *fuzzy baseline*. There are two main approaches as to where this information is taken from:

- Traffic sniffing

- Protocol template

Traffic sniffing means that the fuzzer has a sniffer component or knows how to read a sample of a packet capture and generate the input iterations from what it observes being used.

Protocol template means that the fuzzer has at least some previous knowledge about the protocol implementation, and the input iterations are generated from what the protocol specifies. This mostly applies to (and is more known as) *protocol-based fuzzing*, to distinguish from *data-set based* templates.

The *input generation* (which generates *attack vectors* of legal, semi-legal, and completely broken input) is done by the engine using two main approaches:

- Value manipulation
- Protocol manipulation

Value manipulation is what SPIKE, Peach, smudge, and most fuzzers available as open source basically do. It bases the iterations of input generated on the *data-set based* template it is provided with using *block-based fuzzing*.

With SPIKE, for example, this request can become a template:

```
"GET /blah.[] HTTP/1.1"
```

Unrelated to SPIKE, a good example for a template to manipulate is the TCP packet header format:

```
TCP HEADER FORMAT

OCTET 1,2                 Source Port                      (SRC_PORT)

OCTET 3,4                 Destination Port                 (DEST_PORT)

OCTET 5,6,7,8             Sequence Number                  (SEQ)

OCTET 9,10,11,12          Acknowledgement Number           (ACK)

OCTET 13,14               Data Offset (4 bit)+Reserved
                          (6 bit)+Control Flags(6 bit)     (DTO, FLG)

OCTET 15,16               Window                           (WIN)

OCTET 17,18               Checksum                         (TCP_SUM)

OCTET 19,20               Urgent Pointer                   (URP)

OCTET 21,22,23            Options                          (OPT)

OCTET 24                  Padding

OCTET 25,26…              Data
```

As an example for the preceding, we may choose to send a legal TCP packet and manipulate one field to be malformed, such as the source port (SRC_PORT), which could be a negative number, a number higher than the allowed range as specified in the RFC, etc.

Pre-chosen fields are being manipulated. These are then being manipulated *mainly* for field length and allowed input-type (such as a character vs. a Boolean value vs. an integer vs. a real value, etc.), and so on.

Protocol manipulation is a new technique that currently only seems to be available mainly in commercial products. It is based on the engine having a previous knowledge of the *protocol specification*, beyond the *data-set templates* of *Value manipulation*. (Some open source products use multiple data-set templates to individually fuzz different aspects of a protocol, independently of one another. This is not protocol-based fuzzing).

For example, if the engine knows what HTTP looks like, it can then proceed to create input iterations such as:

```
"GET GET GET blah.blah HTTP/1.1"
"GET /blah.blah /blah.blah FFFFFFFFFFFFFFFFFFFFFFFFFFFFFFF"
```

The *application monitoring* tells the fuzzer whether it was successful (*pass* or *fail*). After all, unless the fuzzer knows that an input sent caused a crash or another similar error, the whole exercise is pointless.

Application monitoring can vary from a watchdog that sees if the program is still running, to a remote check to see if the service is still available and responding, all the way to more advanced techniques like watching with a debugger for an anticipated exception.

Where fuzzing does become almost magical is by its actual capability to provide results. As fuzzing is based on generating often-random data as input until something actually happens (visualize while(1)), it can potentially run for eternity without ever causing a program crash.

NOTE

The bottom line: What differentiates fuzzers is their capability to cause that crash.

The difference between fuzzers begins with their approach to fuzzing, as discussed previously.

Traffic Sniffing

Network sniffers only see traffic that was generated by a client communicating with a server. Whatever their engine may be able to produce, if a certain part of the protocol was never used it would never be tested, which is why they are likely to cover a *significantly small* part of the possible input iterations for the protocol space to find potential vulnerabilities. After all, you don't know what you don't know—and it's those "dark" sections of the protocol implementation nobody ever thinks about where the cruel bugs are hiding.

Prepared Template

Based on the prepared template, the fuzzer may lack some information about what the traffic generated by the implementation tested looks like. However, its Achilles heel is that running over the entire space of possible input iterations can take a significant amount of time, if not forever, especially if the template is a protocol-based representation rather than a simple data-set template for value manipulation.

Further differences between the efficiency of fuzzers are determined by the algorithms used to create the input iterations.

- If *value manipulation* is used, only a specific data-set template can be tested and only for specific value changes.

- If *protocol manipulation* is used, only the protocol structure implementation is tested. However, fuzzers that implement *protocol manipulation* often also implement *value manipulation*. How these are used and if they are combined will eventually determine how successful the attack iterations will be.

Beyond that point, many different technologies and techniques can be used, but they are based on these basic ones. The main difference between fuzzers using all these technologies and techniques would be what types of combinations they would produce, what algorithms would be used, and how efficient the engine would be.

It is often impressive how a fuzzing engine can fuzz something new, mostly without requiring new algorithms or tricks but only the fuzzing baseline to base itself on.

Using *protocol-based fuzzing* certainly takes the field to the next level, but there are many other advances achieved over the last year with the introduction of second-generation fuzzing.

Second-Generation Fuzzing

In the past year, with the introduction of second-generation fuzzing by commercial companies, major advancements in fuzzing have occurred.

These advances begin where we left off at the previous paragraph, with the wide acceptance and success of *protocol-based fuzzing*.

The rest of the advances brought forth by second-generation fuzzing are divided into two main categories:

- Robustness
- Technical advances

Robustness

Robustness simply means the fuzzer is stable. These new fuzzers, unlike some of the early tools, don't crash every few minutes (or seconds) and actually deliver results (i.e., find vulnerabilities).

By far, the field of fuzzing has been dominated by either academic research or homegrown tools developed by researchers to perform specific tasks. As interesting and important to the development of this field as these early efforts were, they were just that, early and perhaps at times even amateurish. This in turn slowed the wide adoption of these tools.

Technical Advances

Learning from the early fuzzing tools, the second-generation fuzzers use protocol manipulation as a framework for their operations. They add value manipulation on top of that to iterate more combinations of attacks to find more potential vulnerabilities ("successful" *test cases*, meaning a *pass* result).

Attacking the way the protocol is implemented is the next step second-generation fuzzers are taking.

Being able to attack the actual implementation of the protocol by generating *attack vectors* that target basic coding errors such as mishandling of input validation or boundary checking (defensive programming errors), design flaws (logical, design specification, and similar), and the implementation of the protocol itself, is how these fuzzers achieve better results.

The main problem with that is that the amount of possible attack combinations increases by a significant factor, making the time-to-result (crash or similar) impractical in some cases. This problem is solved by using advanced algorithms in an attempt to utilize attacks that are more likely to cause an error first, and then proceed to cover the entire combination space.

Still, these algorithms are not easy to develop. On some occasions, trying to exploit a large buffer or to send input of the wrong data-type makes for easy catches, but the more the fuzzer advances in its search, the more significant the efficiency of the algorithms used by individual fuzzers matters.

The use of more advanced manipulations based on the basic two types (*value manipulation* and *protocol manipulation*) also considerably impacts the capability of today's fuzzers to provide results. For example, trying to exploit a logical flaw in the program by sending a login request twice and then combining it into the melting pot of attacks increases the number of combinations required, and the success rate (*pass* results to the tests).

Being able to work with more advanced protocols, requiring the fuzzer to wait for a response before sending the next request (basically establishing sessions with the attacked application—*session-based fuzzing*) is another step in fuzzing.

Some more advanced manipulation techniques based on the basic sets further increase bottom-line results and the success of the fuzzing. One such advanced technique is *logic manipulation*. Based on *protocol manipulation*, the fuzzer attempts to find logical programming errors resulting in a potential vulnerability. An example would be a login request sent twice, or in SMTP, RCPT-TO: being sent before EHLO.

Another advanced technique is *session manipulation* (also based on *protocol manipulation*), which manipulates the actual session. For example, sending a request for a key to be issued, and then when it is received using another one or proceeding without it can cause other types of potential errors.

The main challenge faced by second-generation fuzzers when they employ these new techniques is the time required to cover the combination space exhaustively.

Some exotic vulnerabilities in a product can be located at the very end of the combination space. Developing the technology to try to find the most likely *attack vectors* to trigger likely vulnerabilities in the shortest time possible is critical.

A good example for a vulnerability hiding in a not-often used function is the IIS ISAPI printer extension vulnerability (CVE-2001-0241) from 2001.

Although a vulnerability may still hide at the very end of the combination space and it is important to eliminate it during the test rather than wait for an attacker to do the same, efficiency is an issue.

As a fuzzer can potentially run over the protocol space for eternity, the time frame within which a vulnerability will be found needs to be practical.

There are several technological solutions currently in use to handle this issue. One is the *80/20 rule*.

The *80/20 rule* stands for "Fuzzing What Counts, First." Employing the *80/20 rule* means combinations likely to cause an error are tried first, and the fuzzer advances to explore less likely and more complex *attack vectors* as it advances through the combination space. Further, as new attack vectors are being attempted, they can be organized by *buffers-based* (or *branches-based*) *fuzzing*, from most likely to least likely following the same standard.

Another interesting technique is the application of distributed computing for the use of fuzzing (*distributed fuzzing*). After exhausting some of the smarter algorithms for fuzzing, brute force became the next viable option. Using the power of distributed computing, the fuzzing jobs can be divided between different attacking clients and servers (depending on resources and software capability on both ends), covering more of the combination space in a significantly shorter time frame.

File Fuzzing

Fuzz testing as a concept speaks of input and its manipulation. Much like with network protocols where the fuzzed program can be a client or a server, applications that take files as input can also be fuzzed.

When speaking of file fuzzing, there are two considerations:

- Handling of the file itself
- The standard under which the file is built

For the first, a prime example would be a ZIP archive. If the ZIP file is too large for the application to be able to handle, an error may occur.

For the second, different parts of the file, whether the header in a Windows PE binary or some field in a DOC file, could be malformed.

In some cases, applications could be fuzzed in many different ways. A Web browser could be fuzzed using file fuzzing (loading files such as HTML) and client fuzzing (having it connect to a server that will feed it malformed data).

Host-side Monitoring

As a best practice when fuzzing, the use of a debugger to catch exceptions in the fuzzed application is suggested. There are some other ways to monitor applications, some of which are now being developed on the forefront of fuzzing technology, including:

- Using a profiling and code coverage tools
- Monitoring for memory leaks
- CPU usage and memory usage monitoring

All can help fine-tune the fuzzing process, and assist in pinpointing the vulnerability point in the investigation that will follow.

Vulnerability Scanners as Fuzzers

Vulnerability assessment tools are considered by some to do a similar job as fuzzers do, but of a very basic form. Much like with stress testers, they make for rather primitive fuzzers.

They do not mutate or create any iteration of *attack vectors* other than what was predetermined for them to do in a bounded-group of *test cases*. Stress testers as another example would only check for the stability of the application, and how much input it can handle.

Scanners such as Nessus are efficient at mapping a computer or a network of computers for known vulnerabilities—if a vulnerability is already known, a scan for it will detect whether you are vulnerable, and for example, let you know whether you need to update your software or risk attackers breaking in.

In some cases, tools such as Nessus have been known to trigger vulnerabilities in a new application unrelated to the one they were originally built to exploit. Still, as much as these tests are a good basic test for an application, they do not attempt to exploit it specifically unless they already *know* of a vulnerability for it that was released to the public.

Other similar scanners are *test case based*. These may not attempt to trigger known vulnerabilities, but rather *test cases* known to have caused problems in other implementations of the same protocol in the past. These provide a good basic indication as to the security of the tested software, but do not guarantee (or offer) in any way to test the application being scanned for new, yet unknown vulnerabilities ("0-days").

Uses of Fuzzing

At its most basic, fuzzing is used for black-box testing. What that testing is, what it is used for, and by whom are the main differences.

Fuzzing can be used for anything from stability and reliability testing, to security auditing, to QA security testing during development—any place code is developed and for anyone who touches code.

Fuzzing can be used for and by:

- Automated QA security
- Vulnerability research
- Product testing
- Vulnerability testing before deployment
- Testing third-party products
- Auditors
- Developers

Where programs are being developed and security is a concern, fuzzing can be used as a low-cost and efficient alternative or supplement.

Open Source Fuzzers

There are many open source fuzzers available. These are either built for a specific protocol, or are a framework with which one can develop modules for fuzzing specific protocols.

We cover several open source fuzzing tools later in the book.

For lists of available fuzzers, visit:

- www.scadasec.net/secwiki/FuzzingTools
- www.infosecinstitute.com/blog/2005/12/fuzzers-ultimate-list.html

Commercial-Grade Fuzzers

Commercial fuzzing is a new market trend. Several vendors announced commercial products that are supposed to use some of the advanced techniques described earlier, and their own proprietary technologies, to reach the goal of automated black-box software security testing by the use of fuzzing, and reaching results.

These different vendors employ several different approaches and techniques, diverting from the main ones described previously (*traffic sniffers*, *protocol-based fuzzing*, etc.).

Open source fuzzing today still provides interesting tools and frameworks with which to work, but does not at this point stand at par with what some of the commercial products have to offer.

There are some in-house built (homegrown) fuzzing tools developed by specific software vendors, but these are often built for a specific target and are not public.

Three leading vendors in this field today have their own approach to what fuzzing means and how it is done.

Codenomicon

Codenomicon's approach is that bugs should be located in the shortest time possible. Their product searches for a set of predetermined test cases they have found problematic with implementations of a certain protocol. They perform fuzzing to find these test cases, but their product provides a fast way of testing a product's robustness against these (www.codenomicon.com).

Beyond Security

Beyond Security's beSTORM is an exhaustive fuzzer. Although it supports testing for predetermined test cases and tries to exploit more likely vulnerabilities before continuing with the full test, their main objective is to allow for the most complete testing that will cover as much of the protocol space as possible. With beSTORM, it is also possible to write custom modules for proprietary protocols using XML (www.beyondsecurity.com) (demo download available).

muSecurity

muSecurity's mu4000 uses the man-in-the-middle or proxy approach; it sits on the network, learns the traffic, and tries to manipulate the traffic in a way that will trigger a vulnerability (www.musecurity.com).

What Comes Next

In the future, fuzzers will become much more advanced in regard to what techniques they use. Further, as experience is gathered by their authors, the algorithms for these techniques will be fine-tuned for a much higher success rate and efficiency.

New techniques to use *application monitoring* (also known as *host monitoring*), and different types of *network monitoring*, will be implemented to find new types of vulnerabilities and to optimize the current techniques.

The Software Development Life Cycle

With vendors announcing new fuzzing products every few months during 2006 and the increased awareness of different software companies for the need for security, fuzzing seems to be right on target.

Today, there are limited options for vendors to test their software:

- Secure coding education for their developers
- Source code and static analysis tools
- Vulnerabilities being found and exploited once the product is in the market

None of these options is perfect, and neither is fuzzing. The main difference is that the preceding techniques require a significant investment of resources.

Whether in eliminating false positives, educating staff, or handling patching (development, technical support, and PR) costs, fuzzing offers an alternative that is automated and requires little to no human interaction until the point the error is found.

One of the interesting things about fuzzing is that under normal running conditions, fuzzers have no *false positives* in what they *do* find. Meaning, when an error is received it may not be an exploitable vulnerability, but something bad did happen with the code that at the very least affected the *software stability*, such as a DoS attack.

Fuzzing as a black-box testing field, in our opinion, is going to turn into a significant portion of the vulnerabilities and software/application security markets from all ends, prevention to countermeasures.

Fuzzing is not a perfect solution and it isn't the silver bullet, but when done efficiently it can help eliminate many vulnerabilities in the code space and provide a return-on-investment that far outweighs its implementation costs.

Although fuzzing stands by itself as an efficient software testing technique, it is indeed not the silver bullet. Using fuzzing together with other techniques such as static analysis, whether in the same process or as separate tools, would yield better results with more secure applications.

The implementation of fuzzing in the software development life cycle has been accepted by many software development companies, ranging from Microsoft and Cisco, to Mozilla and Redhat.

Chapter 3

Building a Fuzzing Environment

Solutions in this chapter:

- **Basic Tools and Setup**
- **Data Points**
- **Crash Dumps**
- **Fuzzer Output**
- **Debuggers**

☑ **Summary**

Introduction

Fuzzing is a funny thing and often misunderstood. A fuzzer is a tool used to produce a result, not the result itself, although often the development of the fuzzer is treated as the end of the story. The intended result of a fuzzer is to expose some sort of flaw in a software application that can be used to twist the internal workings and application of the operating system. To make the most of the consequences of a fuzzer run, a researcher must be able to gather all the information possible about the state of the application, the output a fuzzer produces, and other seemingly small pieces of information that can prove the difference between a successful exploit discovery and just another software bug. To properly do this, a researcher must have a well-constructed environment that allows the capture of as much useful information as possible. An environment like this is not built by accident; instead, it requires a lot of time and conscious thought first. Although informative steps to build a good fuzzer in a variety of different methods have been discussed, there has yet to be a good document on how to build a good fuzzing environment.

Knowing What to Ask...

Before you configure the operating system or even write a basic tool, the first thing to do is consider the goal or intent of the testing. One of the basic questions to answer first is, what is being tested? The type of code to be tested will have a large impact on how the environment is constructed. Enough information must be gathered to insure any fault uncovered will be able to be diagnosed and repeatable. This is a dangerous line because it is easy to increase the amount of data collected to the point of uselessness. The information overload state has been reached if more time is consumed sifting through the data of a fuzzer run than analyzing the potential flaw and duplicating it.

Several different types of applications can be fuzzed, in many different ways, and a variety of different problems can be uncovered. For the sake of clarity in this chapter, everything will fit into three different classes: local, network, and Web application.

The local class contains everything that does not require network access to test. Examples of this are media players, word processors, and e-mail applications. Although many of these applications have a network client portion, almost all the same code paths can be reached by loading files locally. For instance, an e-mail client can receive e-mail from a server or it can be loaded locally from a file.

The network class contains all the applications and servers that require network access and have no other way to exercise the code branches. Examples of this are DNS servers, Web servers, and operating system network stacks.

Web applications are technically a subset of the network class but have enough unique and special considerations to have their own class. These could be Web applications available on machine on the same subnet, or a hosted application that is not distributed, like Google mail. These are difficult to test because often a debugger cannot be attached if the only feedback that may be received is cryptic error messages.

After determining the goal, the next logical question to answer is, what class is the application? Having a network-based app, such as a Voice over IP (VoIP) softphone, means there is another stream of data to record, all network-based traffic. This is not hard to do with available tools such as tcpdump and Wireshark. The difference between successfully analyzing this traffic and a time sink is finding which packet or string of packets caused the fault and which can be ignored.

Since Web-based applications are under the same type of scrutiny as any other, considerations for this class have to be made when determining how to build a fuzzer strategy. Since these applications are often remotely hosted, they require a way to determine if an error has occurred, how severe it is, and what could be done with it.

The best question to answer is, how do you know if a fuzzer run is not being wasted? A Web server is a good example of this; what simple things can be done to verify that code branches are actually being exercised with the fuzzer and to assure the traffic is not being discarded by an initial input validation function. This can be done with a variety of code coverage techniques like profilers, and problems can be examined and corrected with debuggers. It's kind of like a nightclub: it doesn't matter if you are the best dancer if you can't get past the doorman.

TIP

It is good to trace through a couple of iterations of a fuzzing run to make sure the data created is actually getting parsed and not dropped. This can be done with tools like profilers or even using the trace command of some debuggers.

With these basic questions answered, it time to begin construction of the environment. There are two major schools of thoughts on how to build the underpinnings of a good fuzzer environment, and the distinction is virtualization. Schools of thought may be a polite label; it is more in the area of holy war much like vi versus Emacs.

Some researchers are fans of using native machines as the basis and when necessary connecting with several machines with Ethernet or Wi-Fi. The upside of a native solution is a good strategy considering many fuzzing targets are devices that can't be virtualized. Examples include routers, mobile devices (like cellular phones and mobile media players), and operating systems that can't be or supposed to be virtualized, like VxWorks or Apple's OSX. There is also a problem with new anti-exploitation technology built in to many machines that may make vulnerabilities that may trigger with the same software version on lesser hardware platforms. An example of this technology is the No-eXecute (NX) technology that prevents certain regions of code from executing. If a vulnerability triggers this feature, the operating system may handle it quietly without any notification to the user, which means there may be no indication that the fuzzer was successful.

Other researchers are of the mindset that virtualization is the best path for using a fuzzer. Virtualization tools like VMware, Virtual PC, and xen are among the most popular virtualization solutions. Tools like these offer the capability to have many different operating systems in an easy to manage solution. One of the most useful features of a virtualization tool like VMware is the capability to create snapshots of the state a machine is in and return to that state quickly (Figure 3.1). This is incredibly useful if the fuzzing target requires a certain state. It is also useful for saving time: repeatedly triggering a vulnerability that may cause a machine to continually need to be restarted or rebooted can waste a lot of time waiting for actions to complete. Being able to revert quickly to a saved snapshot can save a lot of time and assure that re-runs of the fuzzer are targeting the same problem in subsequent runs.

The downside of this approach is the limited amounts of targets. Limiting the scope of research to just a virtualized operating system can rule out many devices, like network cards and their drivers. There is also a problem with the way some virtualization solutions run the operating system and the accompanying low-level code. This could cause undetermined and quirky results in the attempts of exploitation.

Figure 3.1 A Typical VMware Setup with Images for a Variety of Operating Systems

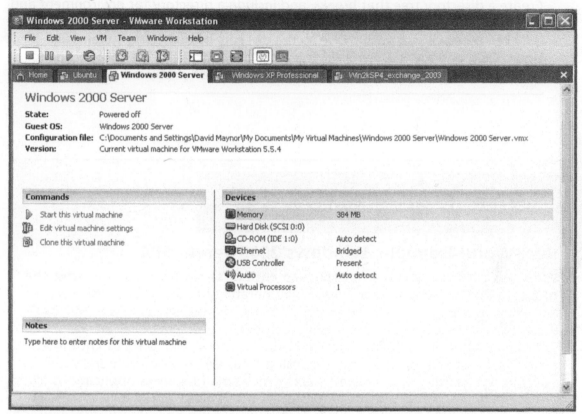

The answer advocated here is that both methods have strengths and weaknesses and should be used where appropriate. For application level vulnerabilities, and even vulnerabilities in basic operating system services, using a virtualization-based solution is timely and efficient. A repeatable test bed is very important, but if a researcher has to spend more time getting the target to run in a VM, a native solution may be better suited.

TIP

Regardless if a virtualization or native OS solution is used, the ability to collect and understand the data rests with the tools used. Tools built in to the operating system can provide the first line of data collection in a fuzzing environment, but are often not up to the task of producing the detailed amount of data required to trace events.

Reliance on third-party tools means that a researcher should create a toolkit that can easily be copied between different machines and even OSes. Create a directory tree that breaks, and include a directory for environment and the necessary tools. The tools for Windows are easy since they are just binaries; they can be stuck in a subdir. Due to the diversity of operating systems like Linux, OSX, and the BSD variants, it is a good idea to keep the source code for those tools in the directories so a quick recompile can produce a working tool.

Tools & Traps…

Real-World Example: Windows 2000 Server SP4

Windows 2000 is a staple in medium to enterprise class businesses across the globe. It is still used as a good basis for vulnerability auditing and discovery for the Windows platform. It is starting to show its age since newer Microsoft applications like Defender or Internet Explorer 7, which means it is best suited for legacy applications. This shouldn't sour a researcher on this choice as a potential platform, because there is still a treasure trove of vulnerabilities in existing applications like Active Directory and small business applications like Great Plains.

A basic set of tools to aid in fuzzer use and vulnerability discovery is comprised mostly of open source or freely available tools like Process Monitor, TCPView, WinDbg, AccessChk, and AccessEnum. WinDbg is used as the primary debugger and has its symbol store set up to automatically retrieve necessary files. WinDbg has also set as the primary post mortem debugger by issuing the `windbg.exe -I` command from a DOS prompt. This means that WinDbg will be launched automatically to examine any crash, which allows a researcher to quickly understand what crashed and why.

Since this is done in a VMware environment, a shared folder is set up with the host OS that contains the tools package and allows for quick sharing of files. This is useful for moving crash dumps, logs, or anything else that should be preserved.

A snapshot is created for every patch rev on the box to allow quick rollbacks. Another snapshot is created when the application to be tested is installed, configured, and verified in the correct working order so a lot of time is not wasted waiting for reboots. Depending on what application is being tested, a variety of system logs like the Event Viewer of crash dump files may need to be retrieved before rolling back to a snapshot.

Tools & Traps…

How a Researcher Makes Use of This Environment

A known vulnerability will be used in this test—CVE-2007-1748—the Microsoft DNS stack overflow. DNS is not essential to the operation of a Windows 2000 box, so crashing the process will result in a hung process at best. A process can be restarted from the Services console under Administrative tools. Since crashing the DNS does not risk crashing the box, Wireshark can be run locally to collect data for later analysis. A simple fuzzer can detect this vulnerability, since it is a stack-based overflow. Process Monitor is also running to record any file reads and writes, and access to any registry keys. This is useful to determine if there is a crash dump and where it is written to.

The fuzzer is designed to stop sending data if the application becomes unresponsive. This ensures that the network logs are not full of data that occurs after the crash and are not essential to tracking down the cause. Figure 3.2 shows the result of the crash and the packet that caused it.

Figure 3.2 WinDbg Analyzing a Crash Dump of a Wireless Driver from a Mobile Phone

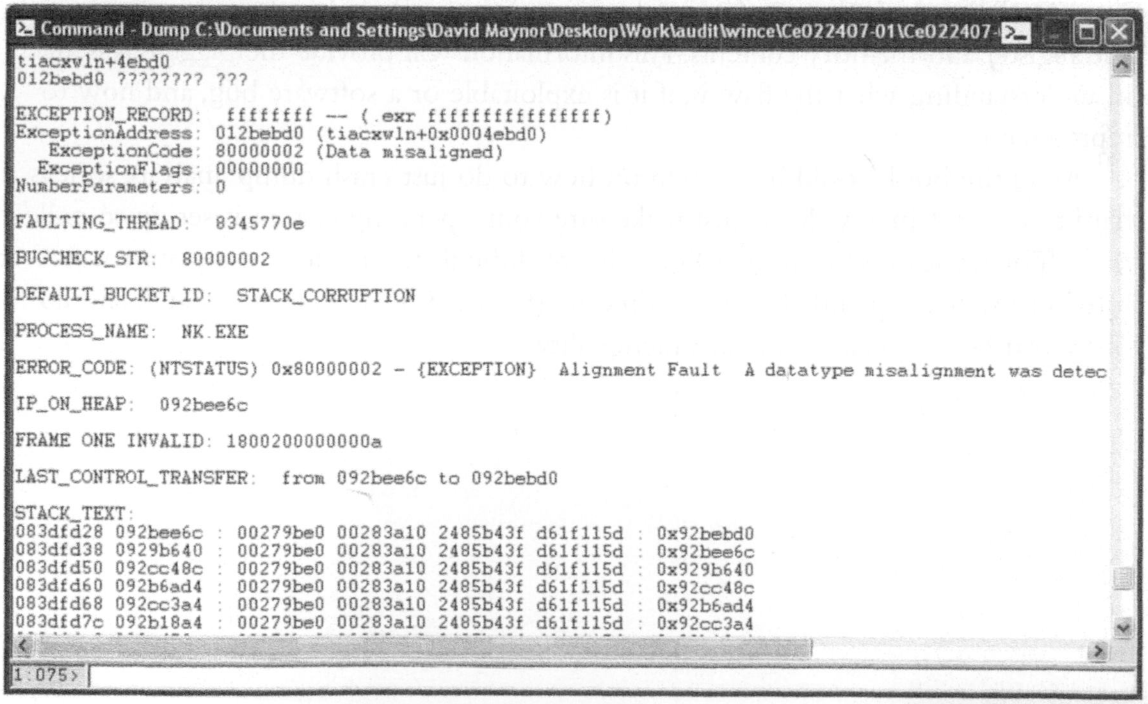

```
Command - Dump C:\Documents and Settings\David Maynor\Desktop\Work\audit\wince\Ce022407-01\Ce022407-
tiacxwln+4ebd0
012bebd0 ???????? ???

EXCEPTION_RECORD:  ffffffff -- (.exr ffffffffffffffff)
ExceptionAddress: 012bebd0 (tiacxwln+0x0004ebd0)
   ExceptionCode: 80000002 (Data misaligned)
  ExceptionFlags: 00000000
NumberParameters: 0

FAULTING_THREAD: 8345770e

BUGCHECK_STR:  80000002

DEFAULT_BUCKET_ID:  STACK_CORRUPTION

PROCESS_NAME:  NK.EXE

ERROR_CODE: (NTSTATUS) 0x80000002 - {EXCEPTION}  Alignment Fault  A datatype misalignment was detec

IP_ON_HEAP:  092bee6c

FRAME ONE INVALID: 1800200000000a

LAST_CONTROL_TRANSFER:  from 092bee6c to 092bebd0

STACK_TEXT:
083dfd28 092bee6c : 00279be0 00283a10 2485b43f d61f115d : 0x92bebd0
083dfd38 0929b640 : 00279be0 00283a10 2485b43f d61f115d : 0x92bee6c
083dfd50 092cc48c : 00279be0 00283a10 2485b43f d61f115d : 0x929b640
083dfd60 092b6ad4 : 00279be0 00283a10 2485b43f d61f115d : 0x92cc48c
083dfd68 092cc3a4 : 00279be0 00283a10 2485b43f d61f115d : 0x92b6ad4
083dfd7c 092b18a4 : 00279be0 00283a10 2485b43f d61f115d : 0x92cc3a4
1:075>
```

Basic Tools and Setup

Although modern operating systems have MANY facilities built in to log operations, they do not provide enough information to locate, debug, and reproduce a crash. To increase the amount of data used and the chance of understanding an uncovered vulnerability, third-party tools are used. Most of these tools are available for download and are often used by application developers to debug or understand how the application actually operates.

Data Points

The data collected is almost as important as the traffic the fuzzer generates. Several different things need to be collected so analysis of a potential flaw can be done easier, and aid in reproduction of the flaw if a problem arises. Many subtle bugs found by fuzzing may require an exact state that happens rarely, or could rely on another application doing something specific.

Crash Dumps

The most important piece of data to collect is the crash dump of the target. Where the crash dump is located and what it contains varies based on the operating system. In general, the crash dump contains the state of the application, the time of the fault, and register and memory contents. This information will provide the biggest assistance in understanding what the flaw is, if it is exploitable or a software bug, and how to reproduce it.

An entire book could be written on how to do just crash dump analysis, so it is hard to cover it in any detail. Just make sure your operating system is set up to collect them. This varies based on the OS but is not difficult to enable. For a platform not listed in the Startup and Recovery Window (Figure 3.3), an Internet search should show you how to enable similar functionality.

Figure 3.3 The Settings for a Crash Dump in Windows

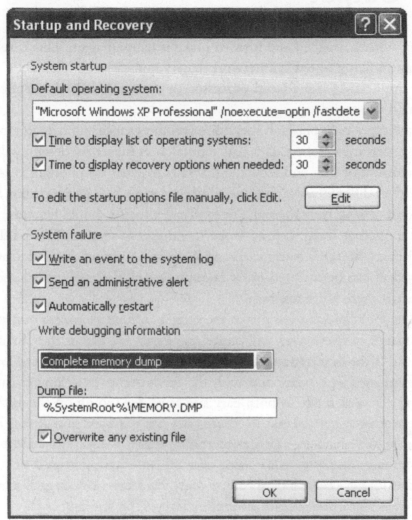

For Linux, enabling crash dumps, called core files on Linux, is just a matter of issuing a *ulimit* command with root privileges. For instance, `ulimit -c unlimited` will allow a core file of any size to be created. Be careful because core files can be very large and use up all the available space on a partition.

A similar command is used in OSX. Adding the line `limit core unlimited` to `/etc/launchd.conf` will enable system core file creation. If the application is being launched from a terminal, you can enable core file creation in just the terminal environment by issuing the same command as Linux, `ulimit -c unlimited`.

Fuzzer Output

Although it may seem obvious, saving the output of a fuzzer is extremely important to diagnosing what happened and how to make it happen again. This is relevant if the application being tested is a network-based application like an RPC server, a host-based application like a word processor, or even a Web-based application like a Web mail front end.

Each of the types of application mentioned requires capturing data in a certain way. One common step among them all is data reduction. A fuzzer, by design, will create a tremendous amount of data, and reducing that data to what is important is essential. This can be handled in different ways, but one simple solution is to develop your fuzzer to interact with the testing environment. For example, a fuzzer should be aware of when its target has crashed or hung, so it no longer continues to send malformed data.

If a third-party fuzzer is being used and it doesn't support that functionality, the data capture tools can be scripted easily enough to poll the application and stop collecting data if there is no response.

Client-side applications are some of the easiest to capture fuzzer output for. Generally, a fuzzer in these cases will create an output file that is then loaded into the application. If the application exits abnormally or hangs, the file can be put aside to be examined in conjunction with the crash dump or debugger output.

Capturing network traffic is both easy and hard depending on the application and how the testing is carried out. Normally, it's just a matter of running a sniffer like tcpdump or Wireshark to capture the traffic, which is easy. The hard part occurs when it comes time to try to make sense of it all. An example would be a hung application that didn't create a crash dump and didn't have a debugger attached. It is hard to determine the state of an application just by looking at its network traffic. Packets could be filtered for a number of reasons such as being malformed, or sent out of order, or at the wrong time. For this reason, its best to always run the target with a debugger attached so information like register contents and what is contained in the stack frame can be captured.

Web applications are a bit different. While running a fuzzer you may not receive any confirmation from the applications that something bad has occurred, not even an error message. Since Web application fuzzing is basically a subset of network-based fuzzing, all the same rules apply. The difference is that the data being recorded may produce a memory corruption problem or flow control issues. The nature and extent of a vulnerability will be hard to judge, especially if it is a hosted application, which makes data collection even more important for the class of fuzzing than the others.

Keeping the fuzzer output has a different side—reusability. In the case of client-side applications like a word processor, all the malformed files created should be kept, to avoid running a similar application over the files that have already been created.

Debuggers

The most important tool used to understand the operation and results of a fuzzer run is a good debugger. Debuggers were developed to allow testing, examination of operation, and debugging in case of a flaw. There are several popular debuggers, each with its own strengths and weaknesses, but in the end the choice of debugger is a personal one and the right tool should be used for the job. Some of the debuggers listed in Table 3.1 are no longer being maintained, or have not been updated in a long time, and some are payware.

Table 3.1 Popular Debuggers

Name	WinDbg.exe
Manufacturer	Microsoft
URL	www.microsoft.com/whdc/devtools/debugging/default.mspx
Description	WinDbg is a versatile debugger produced by Microsoft. It allows for user land debugging, kernel debugging, and crash dump analysis. It can also be set to debug any exception generated on Windows by making it the post-mortem debugger.
Pros	WinDbg is well supported and has great integration with Windows. There is also built-in support for retrieving and loading symbols automatically with the Microsoft symbol server. Kernel mode debugging is also possible with a two-machine setup; LiveKD can be used for single-machine kernel debugging. The trace feature can be used to examine how an application is running, and what code branches are being used. WinDbg's capability to do crash dump analysis is its most useful feature.
Cons	WinDbg is a Windows-only tool with no cross-platform capability. Crash analysis on different machines can lead to incorrect results and incorrect symbol versions being loaded.

Continued

Table 3.1 Continued

Name	Softice
Manufacturer	Compuware
URL	N/A
Description	Softice was one of the best kernel mode debuggers and was extremely useful for all types of debugging tasks. It has been discontinued with no replacement. This means that legacy OSes have great support, but newer operating systems like Windows Vista have no support for it.
Pros	Single-mode kernel debugging.
Cons	Discontinued support.
Name	OllyDbg
Manufacturer	Oleh Yuschuk
URL	www.ollydbg.de
Description	OllyDbg is a disassembler and debugger for Windows operating systems that is focused on binary auditing. It is shareware and is freely available for download. OllyDbg allows for static analysis, and then can be attached to the running process for runtime analysis. Binary patching and a variety of other functionality are built-in.
Pros	Free, powerful, portable, with many features built in. A plug-in development kit allows a researcher to extend the functionality. Highly useful static analysis.
Cons	No kernel debugging and Windows only.
Name	IDA Pro
Manufacturer	Manufacturer: Data Rescue
URL	www.datarescue.com/idabase/index.htm
Description	IDA Pro is the leader in disassembler technology supporting a variety of platforms, processors, and binary types. IDA Pro also contains a debugger that supports a variety of platforms remotely, including Linux, OSX, and Windows Mobile. IDA Pro also supports a powerful scripting language and a plug-in architecture that allows a user-created tool access to any of the IDA Pro functionality.

Table 3.1 Continued

Pros	IDA Pro is the best disassembler on the market with debugger support. Cross-platform support for debugging with a Software Development Kit (SDK) allows researchers to extend the platform's capability.
Cons	The debugger is missing, as are the advanced features of debuggers like WinDbg and Softice.
Name	gdb
Manufacturer	GNU Project
URL	http://sourceware.org/gdb/
Description	gdb is a free, open source debugger that works well on a variety of platforms, including Linux, *nix variants, OSX, and even Windows. It's a powerful and simple debugger that supports many advanced features and can be used remotely for a variety of targets like Cisco's IOS.
Pros	Free, widely accessible, and heavily documented. Gdb supports a wide range of platforms and processor targets. Being open source, a researcher can easily extend its functionality and add research-specific features.
Cons	No official GUI interface, command-line access only.

TIP

The best debugger is a personal choice and depends on an individual's skill level and preferences. My personal choice is a mixture of WinDbg and IDA Pro. WinDbg is used as a primary debugger on platforms that are supported, with IDA Pro used on the remaining platforms. IDA Pro is used for disassembling and binary auditing of all platforms because of the processor, platform, and binary support. Choosing the best debugger will depend on how familiar you are with each tool, and your personal understanding of the low-level operating system internals and your individual needs. If there is no reason to do kernel-level debugging in your project, there isn't much reason to spend a lot of time learning the functionality until you may need it.

In reality, you will find yourself using a variety of these debuggers when certain situations call for it. No matter how much people try, there isn't a single bullet, and staying current with how to use all available tools is the best way to avoid a slowdown in research while you learn how to use something new.

Numerous debuggers are not mentioned here for the sake of space and brevity. The ones listed in Table 3.1 are the most popular to use with fuzzing and the easiest to set up with new systems. Make sure whatever debugger you choose has good support for the target operating system, as research can be set back if a vulnerability is triggered but the debugger in use is not aware of a fault.

Recon Tools

The following is a list of tools, what platform they run on, and what they are best used for. For space concerns, every application useful in a fuzzing environment is not listed, just the most useful.

Windows

Process Monitor

What it does—Process Monitor is a tool from the former Sysinternals group (now owned by Microsoft). It lets a researcher view all reads and writes on a file system and supports filters for data reduction. In addition to the file system activity process, it shows properties such as what modules are loaded, and stack and thread information.

How to use it—Process Monitor is particular useful for discovering log files, crash dump location, and even basic process information like what DLLs are being used.

PsTools

What it does—PsTools is a collection of Windows command-line utilities that allow access to in-depth process information like memory usage and thread information. It can also work remotely so it can be controlled by the fuzzer to determine when applications have had a large processor or memory usage spike.

How to use it—A simple use would be running the command `pslist.exe -s 100000 pid > fuzz.out`, where pid is the targeted application. The value passed to `-s` is the number of seconds the tool should loop. Figure 3.4 shows how simple it is to tell when the application crashed and information about it right before.

Figure 3.4 PsTools Output that Demonstrates What Happens when an Application Crashes During Monitoring

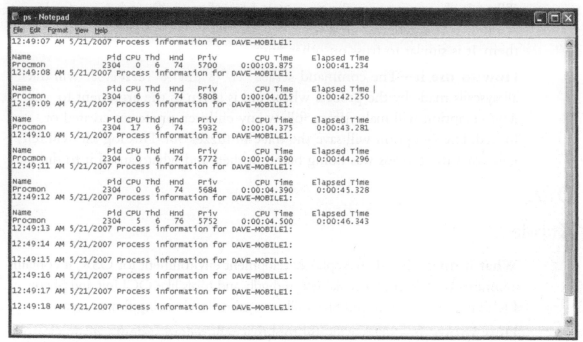

Linux

There are a few useful Linux tools.

Valgrind

What it does—Valgrind is a suite of tools used for memory debugging and code profiling.

How to use it—Different tools in the Valgrind family can help find subtle bugs. Memcheck can detect memory leaks that may lead to a DoS or a race condition, and memory corruption conditions like buffer overflows, off-by-one flaws, and writing to a pointer after it's been freed. This can detect conditions that may not cause a crash but have the potential to do so with properly crafted input.

strace

What it does—strace is the time-tested syscall tracing mechanism for Linux. It allows a researcher to view what system calls are made and the response to them. It is similar to truss on other *nix operating systems.

How to use it—The command `strace -f -p pid -o fuzzer.out` will trace all syscalls made by the process whose pid is given as the argument to -p. The -f option will make strace follow any children processes created or forked. The -o option will save the trace in fuzzer.out. This log file will tell you what the process was doing before it died and what caused it to die.

OSX

Xcode

What it does—Xcode is Apple's development environment for OSX. It contains a number of different tools like gcc and gdb, and tools like OCUnit and Shark. OCUnit is a unit tester, and Shark allows system-level tracing functionality.

How to use it—Shark is useful tool that will record system calls made and memory activity like vm faults.

Tools & Traps...

Real-World Example: Mac OSX 10.4 Kernel Debugging

To properly debug an OSX kernel fault, two machines are needed: one as a debugging host and the other as a target. The machines must be running the same kernel version and have copies of the kernel debugging kit. The debugger used for the remote debugging is gdb with aliases provided by Apple. Debugging can occur over Ethernet or FireWire. The setup is relatively painless and involves setting up a static arp entry, creating the necessary symbols, and setting the appropriate boot flags in the target machine firmware. The steps can be found at http://developer.apple.com/DOCUMENTATION/Darwin/Conceptual/KernelProgramming/build/chapter_18_section_5.html.

In addition to the kernel debug tools, Shark is also running. When an application or the OS dies unexpectedly, the crash reporter process will create a file in /Library/Logs/CrashReporter with a corresponding filename. For instance, if Firefox dies, you will find a log called firefox-bin.crash.log. If there is an operating system level crash, a file called panic.log will be created.

To maintain a good testing environment, OSX is installed to an external FireWire drive from which the Macbook can boot. This allows patches to be tested and rolled back without risking losing an environment to reproduce vulnerabilities. The FireWire driver doesn't need to be big; in this setup, it is 40GB with two operating system images on it.

The vulnerability targeted in Figure 3.5, the Atheros-based Wi-Fi vulnerability, is the stock Apple driver for Macbooks, CVE-2006-3508.

Figure 3.5 shows the contents of panic.log displaying the results of a driver vulnerability and the subsequent crash.

Figure 3.5 The Atheros-based Wi-Fi Vulnerability Is the Stock Apple Driver for Macbooks, CVE-2006-3508

```
Terminal — vim — 108x34

Sat Jul 15 10:07:18 2006
panic(cpu 0 caller 0x0019C9EF): Unresolved kernel trap (CPU 0, Type 14=page fault), registers:
CR0: 0x8001003b, CR2: 0xa299fe10, CR3: 0x0163d000, CR4: 0x000006e0
EAX: 0x00000006, EBX: 0x25faf00a, ECX: 0xa299fe10, EDX: 0x25faf00a
ESP: 0xa299fe10, EBP: 0x141fbad4, ESI: 0xa299fe16, EDI: 0x25faf069
EFL: 0x00010206, EIP: 0x00195949, CS:  0x00000008, DS:  0xa0b30010

Backtrace, Format - Frame : Return Address (4 potential args on stack)
0x141fb984 : 0x128b5e (0x3bbf84 0x141fb9a8 0x131bbc 0x0)
0x141fb9c4 : 0x19c9ef (0x3c13b4 0x0 0xe 0x3c116c)
0x141fba74 : 0x197b8d (0x141fba88 0x141fbad4 0x195949 0x3040048)
0x141fba80 : 0x195949 (0x3040048 0x10 0x10 0xa0b30010)
0x141fbad4 : 0x2b518e88 (0xa299fe10 0x25faf00a 0x6 0x38)
0x141fbb24 : 0x2b50ecb9 (0x2f5e004 0x141fbc8c 0x25faf000 0x50)
0x141fbb84 : 0x2b51f794 (0x2e4346c 0x141fbc8c 0x25faf000 0x50)
0x141fbce4 : 0x2b52fbd4 (0x2e4346c 0x25f79700 0x2e8f004 0x50)
0x141fbd34 : 0x2b5209a0 (0x2e4346c 0x25f79700 0x2e8f004 0x50)
0x141fbe24 : 0x2b530865 (0x2e4346c 0x25f79700 0x2e8f004 0x33)
0x141fbf14 : 0x38d939 (0x2e4329c 0x2e1cc80 0x1 0x12)
0x141fbf64 : 0x38cae5 (0x2e1cc80 0x0 0x0 0x198bf5)
0x141fbf94 : 0x38c809 (0x3500540 0x3500540 0x0 0x8000)
0x141fbfd4 : 0x197a29 (0x3500540 0x0 0x2f96f90 0x25faf00a) Backtrace terminated-invalid frame pointer 0x0
       Kernel loadable modules in backtrace (with dependencies):
          com.apple.driver.AirPortAtheros5424(103.5)@0x2b50d000
             dependency: com.apple.iokit.IONetworkingFamily(1.5.0)@0x2a267000
             dependency: com.apple.iokit.IOPCIFamily(2.0)@0x243c5000
             dependency: com.apple.iokit.IO80211Family(112.1)@0x2b4f4000

Kernel version:
Darwin Kernel Version 8.6.2: Thu Apr 13 18:48:29 PDT 2006; root:xnu-792.9.59.obj~1/RELEASE_I386

*********
```

Summary

The environment of a target process can have a lot of influence on how the process behaves to such a degree it can make the difference between a vulnerability being found and a lot of time being wasted. A good environment should provide a researcher the ability to repeat tests easily and monitor the test.

The ability to record fuzzer data and process state is just as important as the construction of the fuzzer itself. A variety of tools can be used for this purpose on a number of different platforms. The most important tool in researchers' toolkits are a good debugger and the ability to go through crash dumps. The insight a debugger gives on the operation of a fuzzer target combined with the state information found in the crash files provides a detailed roadmap for duplicating a crash, analyzing it, and developing the flaw into an exploit.

The tools used to capture the data may change between different platforms, but the type of data you want to collect doesn't. The fuzzer output, any network logs, and as much state information about the target is the most valuable data to collect.

## Chapter 4

Open Source Fuzzing Tools

Solutions in this chapter:

- **Fuzzing Frameworks**
- **Special-Purpose Tools**
- **General-Purpose Fuzzers**

Introduction

Fuzzing tools typically fall into one of three categories: fuzzing frameworks, special-purpose tools, and general-purpose fuzzers.

Fuzzing frameworks are good if you are looking to write your own fuzzer or need to fuzz a customer or proprietary protocol. The advantage is that the tool set is provided by the framework; the disadvantage is that all open source fuzzing frameworks are far from complete and most are very immature.

Special-purpose tools are usually fuzzers that were written for a specific protocol or application. While they can usually be extended, they are fairly limited to fuzzing anything outside the original scope of the project. In addition, in many cases general-purpose fuzzers are very partial, as the writers tend to use them to find a few holes in a protocol/application and then move on to more interesting things, leaving the fuzzer unmaintained.

General-purpose tools are neat, if they work. They typically don't, and those that do are too general and lack optimization to be very useful.

However, the existence of open source fuzzers is a good starting point to start fuzzing with minimal effort, and to get ideas on how fuzzing should be done and how it works.

The following list is an almost complete compilation of open source tools. Only tools whose source code is accompanied with the binary form, or have a source code version of them, are listed here.

Frameworks

Fuzzing frameworks will help you write your own fuzzer.

Peach Fuzzer—http://peachfuzz.sourceforge.net/

From the Web site: "Peach is a cross-platform fuzzing framework written in Python. Peach's main goals include: short development time, code reuse, ease of use, and flexibility. Peach can fuzz just about anything from .NET, COM/ActiveX, SQL, shared libraries/DLLs, network applications, Web, you name it."

Peach is one of the more advanced open source fuzzing frameworks available. Peach has a framework to do your own fuzzing or extend it by adding code to it. It includes many external interfaces to encryption functions, compression libraries, and encoding types.

(L)ibrary (E)xploit API – lxapi— http://lxapi.sourceforge.net/

From the Web site: "A selection of python methods designed for bug testing and exploitation of local and remote vulnerabilities. It includes a fuzz testing component, miscellaneous shellcode methods and a simple GUI."

The tool appears to have been dropped around the year 2003 and is no longer maintained. In addition, at the time of writing the ZIP file found on sourceforge appears to be broken.

Autodafe—http://autodafe.sourceforge.net/

From the Web site: "Autodafe is a fuzzing framework able to uncover buffer overflows by using the fuzzing by weighting attacks with markers technique."

Autodafe supports fuzzing of both network and file standards, and reverse roles fuzzing, where instead of fuzzing against a server, it is able to perform fuzzing against a client connecting to it ("client-side fuzzing"). Unlike other fuzzers, Autodafe is able to take a pdml file (an XML-based packet dump) and generate the structure the fuzzer will use to perform the fuzzing. This saves a lot of time, as it works around the need for you to teach Autodafe how your server communicates.

The tools haven't changed since August 2006 and appear to be unmaintained.

RIOT and faultmon—http://media.wiley.com/ product_ancillary/83/07645446/DOWNLOAD/ Source_Files.zip

A proof of concept type of tool that can interpret provided data and change its content by looking for specific markers such as equal, bigger than, and ampersand characters. It can be used for testing plaintext protocols such as HTTP, SMTP, POP3, etc.

Scratch—http://packetstormsecurity.org/UNIX/ misc/scratch.rar

From the Web site: "Scratch is an advanced protocol destroyer ("fuzzer") which can routinely find a wide variety of vulnerabilities from a simple packet. Scratch does complex parsing of binary files to determine what to fuzz with what data. Scratch also comes with a framework for fuzzing binary protocols such as SSL and SMB."

Scratch is a fairly simple fuzzer framework that supports both binary and textual fuzzing of data. Scratch "understands" simple elements such as halfwords (BYTE), words, big endian, little endian, and variables and blocks.

antiparser—http://antiparser.sourceforge.net/

From the Web site: "antiparser is a fuzz testing and fault injection API. Fuzz testing has application as a security research methodology and for software quality assurance purposes."

antiparser implements two methods of fuzzing: *random*, where it generates a random fuzzed state and sends it, brings back the data to its original form and tries again; and *increment,* where it generates malformed data from the top of the data to the bottom sequentially. The random works well, while the incremental appears to be broken and not fully implemented.

The tool hasn't changed since August 2005 and appears to be unmaintained.

dfuz—www.genexx.org/dfuz/

From the Web site: "dfuz is a remote protocol fuzzer/triggerer which can do many things such as sending random data/random sizes, together with the data you want. It has a lot of ways to tell the program to use this data by using rule files which will be later parsed by the program itself, and with several options and ways to make it very specific, and very flexible. It's not only a remote protocol fuzzer as itself, but it is a scripting-like motor on which you can create any kind of payload, user-friendly."

dfuz is a generic fuzzing framework. It receives rules, which are used to generate a protocol that can then fuzz a product. dfuz also includes several protocol interfaces that allow quicker testing of SMB- and RPC-based protocols.

The tool hasn't changed since June 2006 and appears to be unmaintained.

Special-Purpose Tools

These tools are generally fuzzers written for a specific protocol or application. While they can usually be extended, they are fairly limited to fuzzing anything outside the original scope of the project.

fuzz—http://pages.cs.wisc.edu/~bart/fuzz/fuzz.html

From the Web site: "Fuzz testing is a simple technique for feeding random input to applications. While random testing is a time-honored technique, our approach has three characteristics that, when taken together, make it somewhat different from other approaches."

fuzz was for many years the only fuzzer available. It was built as part of the academic work done by the University of Wisconsin.

SPIKE Proxy—www.immunitysec.com/ resources-freesoftware.shtml (Web applications)

From the Web site: "Not all Web applications are built in the same way, and hence, many must be analyzed individually. SPIKE Proxy is a professional-grade tool for looking for application-level vulnerabilities in Web applications. SPIKE Proxy covers the basics, such as SQL Injection and cross-site-scripting, but it's completely open Python infrastructure allows advanced users to customize it for Web applications that other tools fall apart on. SPIKE Proxy is available for Linux and Windows."

SPIKE Proxy is a "twist" on SPIKE—it uses a MiTM ("man in the middle") approach, which means it receives input (usually live input) on one side and "spits" out malformed data on the other side by altering its content.

This makes SPIKE Proxy seamless to use and requires very little configuration or customization to the fuzzer itself, rather only the traversing of the Web site while SPIKE Proxy is set as the Web browser's proxy server.

The tool hasn't changed since August 2005 and appears to be unmaintained.

AxMan—www.metasploit.com/users/hdm/ tools/axman/ (ActiveX)

From the Web site: "AxMan is a Web-based ActiveX fuzzing engine. The goal of AxMan is to discover vulnerabilities in COM objects exposed through Internet Explorer. Since AxMan is Web-based, any security changes in the browser will also affect the results of the fuzzing process. This allows for a much more realistic test than other COM-based assessment tools. AxMan is designed to be used with Internet Explorer 6 only."

AxMan is Metasploit's ActiveX fuzzing engine. It can be used to test any available ActiveX and requires very little intervention to do the testing itself, as it uses Internet Explorer as the interface to the ActiveX. The program is known to have found several issues in commercial ActiveXes.

Mangle—http://lcamtuf.coredump.cx/ - HTML file fuzzer

From the Web site: "A trivial utility to automatically check for HTML parsing flaws. Generates a basic set of badly mangled tags on request, with auto-refresh back to the script, so that you can point a browser to it once, and let it run until it crashes."

The program is fairly simple to understand and use. It contains a list of HTML keywords, tags and special characters to use, and includes an instruction at the top for the browser to refresh the page as soon as it's "ready" (a delay of zero).

This program is known to have found issues in various browsers, including Opera, Mozilla, Lynx, Internet Explorer, and Links. Several of the issues discovered by the tool and its variants were used by worm writers (Bofra worm—IFRAME issue) to spread themselves.

The tool is no longer maintained.

screamingCobra—http://samy.pl/scobra/README.txt (Web applications)

From the Web site: "Any CGI that doesn't check arguments that are passed to it over the Web are possibly vulnerable to attacks which allow a malicious user to get read access to almost any file on that system, if not access to execute programs. screamingCobra is almost always able to find those bugs *remotely* due to the common errors programmers make.

screamingCobra is an application for remote vulnerability discovery in *any* *unknown* Web applications such as CGIs and PHP pages. Simply put, it attempts to find vulnerabilities in all Web applications on a host without knowing anything about the applications. Modern CGI scanners scan a host for CGIs with known vulnerabilities. screamingCobra is able to "find" the actual vulnerabilities in *any* CGI, whether it has been discovered before or not."

Unlike other Web testing tools, screamingCobra tests for just two types of Web attacks: directory traversal and command execution, and both only for Unix systems.

The product hasn't changed since January 2002 and appears to be unmaintained.

WebFuzzer—http://gunzip.altervista.org/ g.php?f=projects#webfuzzer (Web applications)

From the Web site: "WebFuzzer is a tool that can be useful for both pen testers and Web masters, it's a poor man's Web vulnerability scanner."

WebFuzzer is a more mature Web fuzzer than screamingCobra, and is able to test for SQL injections, directory traversal, cross-site scripting, and command execution vulnerabilities. However, just like screamingCobra, the tool's functionality is very limited. As you cannot control what it fuzzes—for example, the tool crawls through the Web site on its own—you can't make the tool authenticate against the Web site.

The product hasn't changed since December 2004 and appears to be unmaintained.

ip6sic—http://ip6sic.sourceforge.net/

From the Web site: "ip6sic is a tool for stress testing an IPv6 stack implementation. It works in a way much similar to isic. It was developed mainly on FreeBSD and is known to work on OpenBSD and Linux. Theoretically, it should work wherever libdnet works."

It is hard to state that ip6sic is a fuzzing tool, as its aim appears to be more in the realm of stress testing than fuzzing, but it does generate malformed data and valid in an attempt to cause the IPv6-enabled device to misbehave.

The tool hasn't changed since October 2003 and appears to be unmaintained.

BlueTooth Stack Smasher (BSS)—www.secuobs.com/ news/05022006-bluetooth10.shtml

From the Web site: "BSS (Bluetooth Stack Smasher) is a L2CAP layer fuzzer, distributed under GPL license."

BlueTooth Stack Smasher (BSS) is an easy-to-use BlueTooth fuzzer. It can generate a variety of L2CAP packets, including L2CAP_COMMAND_REJ, L2CAP_CONN_REQ, L2CAP_CONN_RSP, L2CAP_CONF_REQ, L2CAP_ CONF_RSP, L2CAP_DISCONN_REQ, L2CAP_DISCONN_RSP, L2CAP_ ECHO_REQ, L2CAP_ECHO_RSP, L2CAP_INFO_REQ, L2CAP_INFO_RSP, and arbitrary data structures that are then sent to the BlueTooth listening device.

Radius Fuzzer—www.suse.de/~thomas/projects/ radius-fuzzer/

Radius Fuzzer is a RADIUS protocol fuzzing tool. Its fuzzing is not limited to format strings, and will also try to generate malformed packets that contain SQL injections, cross-site scripting, and command execution. Curiously, it doesn't try to manipulate the relationship between length and values found inside the RADIUS packets. The fuzzer also doesn't include code that determines if the SQL injection, cross-site scripting, and command execution attacks were successful.

The tool hasn't changed since September 2005 and appears to be unmaintained.

COMRaider—http://labs.idefense.com/software/fuzzing.php

From the Web site: "COMRaider is a tool designed to fuzz COM Object Interfaces."

COMRaider eases the fuzzing process of COM objects, namely ActiveXes. It has a nice user interface, is easy to use, and requires very limited know-how of the ActiveX being tested, as it can automatically detect the methods and attributes the ActiveX exports and fuzz them.

fuzzball2—www.nologin.net/main.pl?action=codeView&codeId=54&

From the Web site: "fuzzball2 is a little fuzzer for TCP and IP options. It sends a bunch of more or less bogus packets to the host of your choice."

fuzzball2 is a TCP and IP packet fuzzer; it can send various malformed packets and play with the options defined inside the TCP and IP packet structure.

The tool hasn't changed since April 2005 and appears to be unmaintained.

General-Purpose Tools

General-purpose tools are a good beginning to fuzzing with minimal effort, and to get ideas on how fuzzing should be done and how it works.

TAOF—www.theartoffuzzing.com/joomla/index.php?option=com_content&task=view&id=16&Itemid=35

From the Web site: "TAOF is a GUI cross-platform Python generic network protocol fuzzer. It has been designed for minimizing set-up time during fuzzing sessions and it is especially useful for fast testing of proprietary or undocumented protocols."

TAOF is the first GUI-based fuzzer that tries to ease the process of fuzzing new and unfamiliar protocols by allowing you to mark the sections of the data you are interested in testing. TAOF is able to test overflows and length value relationships—where a length is larger or smaller than the provided value.

SPIKE—www.immunitysec.com/resources-freesoftware.shtml

From the Web site: "When you need to analyze a new network protocol for buffer overflows or similar weaknesses, SPIKE is the tool of choice for professionals.

While it requires a strong knowledge of C to use, it produces results second to none in the field. SPIKE is available for the Linux platform only."

One of the first block-based open source fuzzing tools, it has been presented at several BlackHat conferences and has received numerous mentions in the press. SPIKE is known to have found issues in Microsoft Windows' RPC framework and other products.

The tool hasn't changed since August 2005 and appears to be unmaintained.

FileFuzz—http://labs.idefense.com/software/fuzzing.php

From the Web site: "FileFuzz is a graphical Windows based file format fuzzing tool. FileFuzz was designed to automate the executing the launching of applications and detection of exceptions caused by fuzzed file formats."

FileFuzz takes sample files, which it uses for its fuzzing. Its fuzzing methodology is mainly focused on modification of bytes found inside the original sample and generating a derivative from them.

FileFuzz also integrates an automated tool for opening all the files it has fuzzed, and detects whether they cause an exception automatically. For those programs that prompt errors, FileFuzz supports an automated process of killing the program after a set time that nothing has happened (no exception has occurred).

SPIKEFile—http://labs.idefense.com/software/fuzzing.php

From the Web site: "SPIKEFile is a Linux based file format fuzzing tool, based on SPIKE 2.9. It was designed to automate executing the launching of applications and detection of exceptions caused by fuzzed file formats."

As the name states, SPIKEFile is an "adaptation" of the SPIKE tool for file fuzzing. It uses the same functionality of block-based fuzzing techniques SPIKE uses, but its output are files.

notSPIKEFile—http://labs.idefense.com/software/fuzzing.php

From the Web site: "notSPIKEFile is a Linux based file format fuzzing tool. It was designed to automate executing the launching of applications and detection of exceptions caused by fuzzed file formats."

notSPIKEFile is another flavor of SPIKEFile, which doesn't use the source code of SPIKE as its base for doing the fuzzing process of files.

eFuzz—http://packetstormsecurity.org/Win2k/ efuzz01.zip

From the product's description: "eFuzz is an easy to use fuzzer (Penetration testing tool) to search for unknown vulnerabilities in software (buffer overflows, format string vulnerabilities, integer overflows, command line overflows,…)."

eFuzz is a simple replacement fuzzer that changes the data you provide it and sends it out to the server being tested; you can create a test configuration and then eFuzz will generate malformed data using them.

The product hasn't changed since November 2004 and appears to be unmaintained.

Blackops Fuzzing Tools—www.blackops.cn/tools/

Blackops fuzzing tools is a collection of fuzzing tools for HTTP, SMTP, FTP, POP3, and Windows Device Drivers. It was written by Ollie Whitehouse.

The tool hasn't changed since December 2005 and appears to be unmaintained.

## Chapter 5

Commercial Fuzzing Solutions

Solutions in this chapter:

- beSTORM (by Beyond Security)

- BPS-1000 (by BreakingPoint Systems)

- Codenomicon

- Mu-4000 Security Analyzer (by Mu Security)

Introduction

As fuzzing becomes more mainstream, there is a real need for commercial tools to help those who need to use fuzzing tools but do not want to "mix-and-match" various free tools that may be half-baked and frequently suffer from lack of maintenance or support. Those who need the tool to "just work" may want to look at the commercial tools available.

The obvious disadvantage of commercial tools (other than costing money) is that you are limited to the vendor's way of doing things. Unlike open source tools, you cannot dive into the code and tailor it to your specific needs.

However, commercial tools tend to have a more complete rationale for how to use them, and usually work "out of the box." Consequently, the money you pay is often saved by the quick path to using or implementing them into your fuzzing process, especially if your interest is beyond a mere hobbyist.

Four commercial products typically are mentioned when it comes to fuzzing, and although some of them do not fit the classic definition of fuzzing, each solves the problem from a different perspective. All products are already mature and proven and are in use by large corporations worldwide.

In the next few years, more commercial solutions are likely to appear as the need for fuzzers grows.

Here are the solutions in alphabetical order.

beSTORM (by Beyond Security)

"beSTORM performs a comprehensive analysis, exposing security holes in your product and during the development process. beSTORM represents a new approach to security auditing. Most of the security holes found today in products and applications can be discovered automatically. By using an automated attack tool that tries virtually all different attack combinations, with the ability to detect certain application anomalies and indicate a successful attack, those security holes can be found almost without user intervention."

beSTORM is both a fuzzing framework and a protocol-specific fuzzer. It comes with a predefined set of protocol "modules," each containing a full description of the protocol according to the RFC. beSTORM attempts to create all the different combinations of the protocols, and sends them to the target. Since every different combination is "fuzzed," beSTORM covers the entire protocol space almost entirely (sample screen shots in Figures 5.1 and 5.2).

Figure 5.1 beSTORM Snapshot

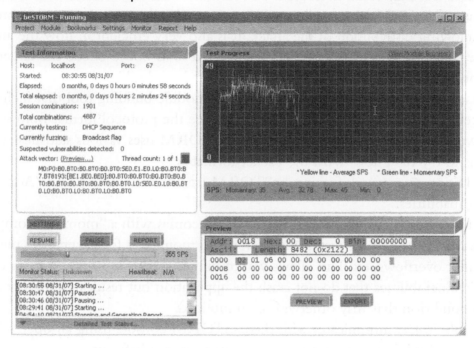

Figure 5.2 beSTORM Snapshot

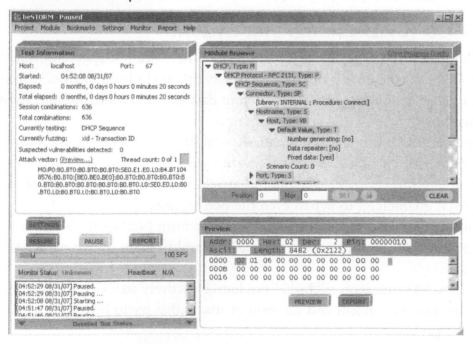

Because this may result in millions and sometimes hundreds of millions of combinations, beSTORM supports parallelism in several ways—by being multithreading and by allowing distribution of the attack. It is also very efficient in how the attacks are done, allowing you to throttle the attack speed so as not to choke the target.

If you would like to extend the protocol module or build a test module for your proprietary protocol, beSTORM comes with a module building tool that includes very nice "auto-learn" capabilities to try to deduce the protocol format from sniffing the network or analyzing captured packets. beSTORM uses various statistical analysis functions to try to "guess" what the packet format is.

In addition to network fuzzing, beSTORM has file fuzzing and DLL/ActiveX fuzzing capabilities.

Finally, to complete the package, beSTORM comes with a "monitor" component that can attach itself to the tested application and monitor it for exceptions, memory leaks, buffer overflows, etc. This allows you to pinpoint the problem and helps catch "subtle" vulnerabilities that do not crash the application but result in a memory overrun condition that may otherwise go unnoticed.

The monitor communicates with the beSTORM console using an open API, which allows building custom monitors for proprietary platforms.

Once a weakness is discovered, beSTORM can generate a Perl script that recreates the problem and can be used by a QA team to further investigate the issue.

BPS-1000 (by BreakingPoint Systems)

"BreakingPoint has developed the most powerful network test system on the planet, the BPS-1000. At the core is our advanced network application engine, with the ability to generate millions of real application data streams, while pushing security to the max.

With over 3,000 unique security attacks and the ability to receive a monthly update of the latest attacks, we can truly verify your equipment is secure. Our ability to generate unique never-seen-before real attacks with an exhaustive list of evasion techniques is guaranteed to bypass even the best security devices."

BreakingPoint System was founded by people from NetWorth, NetSpeed, and TippingPoint, along with the creator of the Metasploit open source penetration testing suite.

The BPS-1000 attempts to "break" products by actively attacking them with known attacks, yet-unknown attacks, and variation of attacks that try to bypass security systems that may be installed on the product. It can be best used to perform a benchmark between security devices (firewalls, IDSs, etc.), as it tries to emulate a hacker attack on the device. However, like the traditional fuzzers, it can also be used by developers to try to find security holes in their product.

BPS-1000 is not an "exhaustive" test and does not necessarily focus on testing the product's security.

However, it is unique, as it will try to perform the attacks in a "stealth" way to try to bypass any security measures that are installed.

The appliance is very suitable for robustness testing, either by creating complicated traffic scenarios or by capturing your own network traffic (in speeds up to 1Gps) and recreating the traffic, altering it, or amplifying it. It is capable of creating millions of TCP sessions, and can create "fuzzed" Ethernet, IP, TCP, or UDP packets similar to the traditional network fuzzers. Twenty protocols are supported, using several thousand prebuilt attacks that are updated periodically.

Codenomicon

"Codenomicon develops and markets state-of-the-art software testing tools for proactive elimination and prevention of security vulnerabilities. Codenomicon test tools are available for a wide range of protocols and file formats."

Codenomicon is the commercial version of the popular PROTOS testing suite. It is not a single product, but separate testing tools available for a wide range of network protocols (Figures 5.3 and 5.4).

Unlike the "classic" definition of a network fuzzer, Codenomicon's testing tools do not arbitrarily fuzz valid requests. Instead, the Codenomicon team built a set of case studies known to be problematic. These case studies try to give a good simulation of all the known security holes of the protocol and their variants. The advantage of this approach is that testing can be done fairly fast, compared to a traditional fuzzer. The number of case studies ranges from thousands to tens of thousands.

Codenomicon seems to focus on application robustness, so their tests attempt to see if the product can "survive" the attacks and continue to provide a useful service. The testing suites are available for both network protocols and file formats ("file fuzzing").

Although there is no way for the user to extend testing modules or create tests for proprietary protocols, PROTOS is still available and can be used for custom or proprietary protocols. The company also seems to be very responsive to new protocol requests and extensions.

At the time of writing, the following protocol testing suites are available:

- Audio (AU, AIFF, AMR, MIDI, iMelody, ID3, MP3, WAV, and VOC)
- BGP
- Bluetooth
- Compression
- Diameter (server)
- DNS (server and client)
- DVMRP
- EAP
- FTP (server)
- GRE
- GTP
- H.248
- H.323
- HTTP (server and client)
- Images (GIF87, GIF89M/A, JPEG/JFIF, MBM, MSBMP, MSICO, PNG12, PCX, PBM, PGM, PPM, RAS, XBM, XPM, and WBMP)
- IMAP (server)
- IPSec
- IPv4 (TCP, UDP, IPv4, ARP, ICMP, IGMP)
- IPv6 (TCP, UDP, IPv6, ICMPv6/MLD)
- ISAKMP/IKE (server)
- IS-IS

- LDAP (server)
- MGCP
- MPLS/LDP
- NTP (both)
- OSPF
- PIM-SM/DM
- POP3 (server)
- RADIUS (both)
- RIP
- RSVP
- RTSP
- RTP
- SigComp
- SIP (both)
- SMTP (server)
- SNMP (server)
- SSH (server)
- TACACS+ (server and client)
- TLS/SSL (server and client)
- Video
- X.509

Figure 5.3 Codenomicon Test Tool

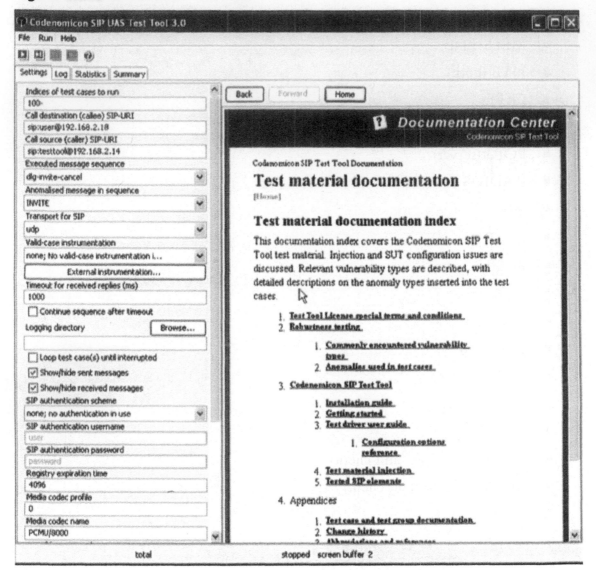

Figure 5.4 Codenomicon Snapshot

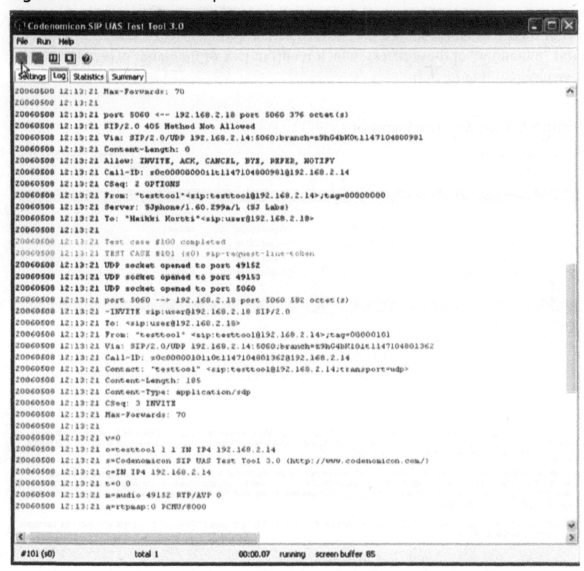

Mu-4000 Security Analyzer (by Mu Security)

"Mu Security is developing solutions to characterize, quantify, and proactively improve security. Using this approach, it is possible to detect unknown and known vulnerabilities in applications and systems by methodically attacking target systems to uncover flaws; compare the relative robustness of different products to malicious attacks; and drive improvement in product security through quantifiable metrics."

The Mu–4000 Security Analyzer is an appliance-based solution that tries to quantify or certify network products. It can be used, for example, by IDS vendors to see if their IDS blocks known attacks on a certain protocol. Mu sends known attacks, and "mutations" of those attacks, which results in tens of thousands of attacks per protocol (Figure 5.5).

Figure 5.5 Mu Security Snapshot

Fault Detail Report

For Box1/FWOS-V2

Overview

	Fault Name	Device	Analysis	Attack Vector Set	Fault Time
1.	DHCP DISCOVER Client ID Option	Box1/FWOS-V2	Firewall 2-22-06	FWTest	2/24/06 7:47 AM
2.	DHCP DISCOVER Client ID Option	Box1/FWOS-V2	Firewall 2-22-06	FWTest	2/24/06 7:44 AM
3.	DHCP DISCOVER Client ID Option	Box1/FWOS-V2	Firewall 2-22-06	FWTest	2/24/06 7:43 AM
4.	DHCP DISCOVER Client ID Option	Box1/FWOS-V2	Firewall 2-22-06	FWTest	2/24/06 7:40 AM

1 DHCP DISCOVER Client ID Option

Details

Appliance	mu4000	Analysis	Firewall 2-22-06	Protocol	DHCP
Device	TestVendor-Box1	Attack Vector Set	FWTest	Suite	DHCP DISCOVER Client ID Option
Software	FWOS-V2	Fault Time	2/24/06 7:47 AM	Variant	Invalid Path in the Client ID Option

Protocol - DHCP

Dynamic Host Configuration Protocol (DHCP) is an application-layer protocol used to dynamically assign IP addresses to network components. DHCP is platform-independent and can configure TCP/IP for multiple operating systems. Typically, a client is configured to run DHCP at startup, when it contacts the DHCP server to obtain an IP address.

DHCP can assign IP addresses from an predefined IP address range or predefined IP pool. A dynamic IP address is assigned for a limited time only; if the client does not renew the assignment lease periodically, the server reuses the address elsewhere. A manual IP address (static address) is assigned permanently (until manually changed). DHCP can also provide other TCP/IP parameters to a client, including subnet mask, gateway, and DNS/WINS settings.

DHCP communications occur over a UDP/IP connection between the server UDP/67 and client UDP/68. DCHP request and response messages use the same packet structure.

An interesting aspect of the testing is the ability to test either the "end point" (a direct attack on the application) or as "pass through." The latter is intended for routers and other network devices, and checks at both ends to analyze what network traffic was sent in by the Mu-4000, and what came out from the device we are testing. This allows checking filtering devices to make sure the right things are being filtered or blocked. It is also a good way to check if things are filtered that shouldn't be; for example, network traffic that is mysteriously altered or blocked by a router.

The Mu-4000 is a 2U rack-mountable appliance that includes four Gb Ethernet and two serial ports, two power sockets for power recycling of systems that lock up during a failure, and both Ethernet and serial management console ports. Being a security appliance, the Mu-4000 provides testing with speed, and the capability to test hardware products by simply connecting them to the testing appliance. The capability to perform a power cycle allows you to run unattended tests for hardware appliances.

## Chapter 6

Build Your Own Fuzzer

Solutions in this chapter:

- What a Fuzzer Should Include
- Fuzzer Building Blocks
- How to Do It
- What a Simple Fuzzer Can Do

☑ Summary

Hold Your Horses

Before we start building a fuzzer, we must understand what a fuzzer is, or at least understand what a fuzzer should include, and why we can't just send in random data. This is also sometimes referred to as the 1/2^32 problem—where in some cases, changing something at random is as good as playing the lottery.

Most people hear the word *fuzzing* or *fuzzer* and immediately imagine something that is obscure, uncertain, or even random. If we look up the phrase "Fuzz testing" in Wikipedia, we see that at least one of the methods of doing fuzz testing is "Simple fuzz usually uses a pseudo random number generator to provide input" (http://en.wikipedia.org/w/index.php?title=Fuzz_testing). Although this approach can yield results, it is uncommon for a random input to cause problems in complicated products.

This is because the probability of someone finding the right bit of data, which will cause a problem in a product that is complicated enough (for example, require authentication or some sort of session handling), is almost impossible or at least improbable.

In theory, we could start sending the product we are interested in testing one byte, and change its value through so that it goes through the value of 0x00 up to the value of 0xFF. Then move to send two bytes of data, and change their value so they pass through 0x0000 up to 0xFFFF. This type of testing, sometimes referred to as a *sequential tester*, will conduct the best fuzz testing possible, but at a very steep price, as you probably could have guessed by now.

This is because it is impractical, as the number of data sets needed to cover a fairly simple data set of the DNS protocol Standard Query, which is 27 bytes long (a query for the host "a"), would take an immensely long time to complete.

NOTE

Even though we refer to protocols, we are not limiting the fuzz-testing field to network protocols. Whenever we refer to a protocol, we are using the term in the context of a "cookbook," the specification or guidelines of how to send data that will be interpreted correctly on the other end.)

To cover all possible combinations of the DNS Standard Query protocol we would in this case send 256^27, which is a very big number—105,312,291,668,557, 186,697,918,027,683,670,432,318,895,095,400,549,111,254,310,977,536—or written in shorter form roughly the number 1 and 65 zeros after it. In computer time, this would be almost infinity; even on a very fast computer able to test millions of combinations per second, it will still take 1 and 60 zeros after it seconds to complete the simple 27 bytes long testing.

We just saw that it is impractical to send every possible combination, even on the simplest protocols. However, what about randomly changing bytes in a given known to be valid data set? Random data changing is a good method to kick start testing of a protocol; it requires no technical expertise or understanding of the protocol.

Two problems arise when randomness is used for fuzz testing, the first being repeatability; the ability for someone to repeat the same random change so the problem discovered can be recreated and investigated. This can be addressed by pre-selecting a fixed random seed so we can recreate the random numbers generated before and after our current position. (Note: Even though we refer to random number, we are actually talking about a pseudo random number, but for sake of clarity, we will not get into the difference between the two.)

However, pre-selecting a fixed random seed does not solve the second issue—protocol integrity. Protocol integrity defines a state where the sender and receiver of the data contained inside the protocol both know how to parse and understand it. The integrity is not always crucial and, in some cases, the un-integrity of the protocol caused by fuzz testing is what we are interested in checking. In many cases, a data set that doesn't stand up to the integrity test will be simply discarded.

Here are some examples:

- A SIP packet not containing the minimal required headers to valid, might trigger a problem in the product being tested, but most SIP parsers will be silently discarded.

- The FTP protocol's command channel, where the USER, PASS, NLST, etc. commands are sent, expects all the data to be printable characters or at the very least not to contain NULL characters or line feeds in the middle of a given command receives such data due to a random change.

- A PE (Portable Executable) file not containing the required initial "MZ" characters will not be regarded as a PE file.

- A ZIP file that was randomly changed without altering the checksum of the file that was modified will not be analyzed.

- Any encrypted data stream would become invalid as soon as we change random bytes of it, as the integrity of the data set would be compromised.

We can provide many more examples, but this isn't the goal of the chapter; rather, we want to understand how we can build our very own fuzzer.

Fuzzer Building Blocks

As we just saw, a fuzzer can't just randomly change data; it has to have some form of understanding what it is changing, as changing it at random in many cases will cause the data to be invalid and discarded without being used by the product being tested.

Therefore, a fuzzer needs:

- One or more valid data sets.

- Understanding of what each byte in that data set means.

- Change the values of the data sets while maintaining the integrity of the data being sent, so it is parsed even if it contains malformed data; for example, maintain the checksum value of a ZIP file.

- Recreate the same malformed data set repeatedly.

- An arsenal of malformed values or the capability to create a variety of malformed outputs (NULL characters, Unicode data, negative values, etc.).

- Maintain a form of a state machine, which will allow us to send an authentication request and use the data returned, if necessary, for subsequent requests.

One or More Valid Data Sets

This building block is used by the fuzzer as the basis for its testing; without it, the fuzzer is no better than our random number generator, or even worse, than our *sequential tester*. This is because we have no way of telling our fuzzer what the known-to-be-good values for the protocol being tested are.

This is especially important for protocols that have fixed values at certain locations, and that these fixed values are used by products to detect the protocol being used.

For example, no Windows ICON file would be processed unless it begins with 0x0000 followed by 0x0100, as the specification clearly states that the file header needs to be:

```
WORD    idReserved;    // Reserved (must be 0)
WORD    idType;        // Resource Type (1 for icons)
```

If we play around with these two first values, the product parsing the ICON file will probably ignore the file loaded and not parse it as an ICON file.

We mentioned that we will need one or more valid data sets, as many protocols have different states (for example, authentication and a request for file listing such as in the case of the FTP protocol), and we can't simply send a file listing request and expect the FTP server to spew the list of files. (Note: In some cases, part of the fuzz testing we are interested in doing is mixing up of the state machine—request a file listing before doing a mandatory authentication procedure. We will not talk about this, as it is less fuzz testing and more logic testing.)

Understanding What Each Byte in the Data Set Means

Simply having a large valid "database" of data sets doesn't mean our fuzzer will know what to do with it. Our fuzzer needs to know and understand what each byte, line, and sequence means. This is very similar to teaching someone a language. We can't just teach him all the possible words, or even complete paragraphs; we must teach how the words are combined into paragraphs, how their meaning changes if we order the words differently, or even change their "value"—adding a *ing* at the end of a verb.

Our fuzzer can be thought of on many levels as how a protocol is defined, from understanding what state comes before what state, to understanding that adding one more character to a certain location requires you to change the length value that precedes it.

In some more common cases we would need to teach the fuzzer to do more than just data manipulation; it needs to know how encoding of data is preformed. This is true whenever things like MD5, CRC32, and Base64 encoding are preformed on the data being sent. Manipulating the value without modifying the corresponding encoded data would cause the data to be invalid and in many cases discarded, whereas modifying and then encoding it would maintain the integrity of the protocol while allowing the fuzzer to test the protocol.

Change the Values of the Data Sets While Maintaining the Integrity of the Data Being Sent

As just mentioned, it is important for the fuzzer to know how to manipulate the data without causing the data to become invalid. Some protocols use a fixed size data set, where, for example, every data set is 512 bytes long, even though variable length values can be stored inside it. This means that some sort of padding, or length and value relationship, needs to be maintained and updated by the fuzzer.

For a fuzzer to be able to do this, it would need to have a list of attributes and characteristics for each byte found inside the protocol. These attributes and characteristics would be applied after the data field is fuzzed.

Recreate the Same Malformed Data Set Time and Time Again

It is already a challenge to find problems with fuzz testing; worse is not being able to understand why they happened or how to recreate them. Imagine this: You kick start your fuzz testing session on a product, leave it overnight, come back in the morning and find out that the program crashed, but unfortunately you don't understand what happened as the program left no trace, and your fuzzer moved on to test other things.

This means that your fuzzer needs to be able to do two things: save a list of last data sets sent to the server, so you can roll back your fuzz testing session to a close proximity to where you were just 10 minutes ago, and be able to pass through the same data sets you have done in those 10 minutes so you would reach the same point you were just at.

This is done for two reasons: you cannot always know which data set caused the issue, and in some cases, a series of data sets can make the program misbehave, usually due to some latent process or task handling causing the crash—usually garbage collectors.

> **NOTE**
>
> Your fuzzer should be able to recreate not only the invalid data set, but also the state machine that brought the protocol to the state of an error. This is true for those protocols that have such requirement of a state machine.)

An Arsenal of Malformed Values, or the Ability to Create a Variety of Malformed Outputs

Wake up any hacker in the middle of the night, ask him what malformed data he would send, and he would say, "buffer overflows—long strings, format strings—percent signs, NULL characters, etc." However, taking that knowledge and converting it to an arsenal that will be used wisely—not sending NULL characters on a textual protocol for example—is no easy feat.

Therefore, your fuzzer needs to have two things: a large set of malformed values, anything from invalid datetime values, through invalid hostname values up to simple long strings, and then each of these malformed values needs to be associated with the fields the fuzzer is going to test.

Here are some examples of groups of malformed values:

- Buffer overflow values A…A (multiple A characters), <<…<<< (multiple smaller than characters), etc.

- Boundary cases like for integer values −2, −1, 0, 2^8-2 = 254, 2^8-1 = 255, 2^8 = 256, 2^12-2 = 4094, 2^12-1 = 4095, 2^12 = 4096, etc., both in literal form (the string representation of −2, −1…) and in encoded form (the binary representation of −2 = 0xFFFFFE, −1 = 0xFFFFFF in a 4-byte field).

- Format strings values %s, %x, %25s—encoded percent, %n, etc.

- NULL character values, either appended to the original data, as standalone data, or removed from the original data (a NULL terminated string no longer being NULL terminated).

- Unicode strings values that include both the Unicode form of the preceding values and malformed Unicode encoded data—data whose Unicode content cannot be parsed as Unicode.

- Off-by-one values, where a length bounded to a string is either one below the true value or one above the true value.

NOTE

Not all malformed values are created equal in the products you test. One malformed value for a product might be a valid one for another; for example, it might disregard the millisecond field provided in the datetime value you provided. Moreover, some products that crash due to 1022 characters being sent to them might not crash upon receiving 1024 characters, as its overflow detection algorithm checks for that value.

Even though a comprehensive arsenal of malformed values is important, exaggerating and making it too large would mean you would probably test much more than needed, or in some cases not be able to test "later" areas (those that occur at the end of the testing phase), as you would be "stuck" at testing the initial parts of the protocol.

It is important to find a balance between a comprehensive arsenal, where the most common issues are tested, and a complete arsenal, where malformed value is tested even if it is irrelevant for the field in question (for example, sending a malformed host value when the protocol specifies that a datetime value should be given).

This balance is best achieved by creating a fuzzer that is able to do a "quick run" where expected values are sent—datetime value sent in the datetime field only, followed by a "probable run," date value sent in the datetime field, finished with a "quick-run" where everything is allowed.

This balanced approach would be the best of both worlds; do a quick test that should find the most probable problems, and the later runs—the "quick run"—should find the more exotic problems.

Maintain a Form of a State Machine

Many protocols, mainly network protocols, require some sort of state machine. Usually, as in the case of the RPC protocol, a binding request is sent, a response is received containing some kind of data field, which should be sent back on any follow-up data sent to the server. In similar fashion to the HTTP protocol where cookies are used to maintain a session, the RPC protocol uses this data—known as the transaction id—to know that the packet being sent to it is part of the same "conversation."

A fuzzer unable to maintain a simple state machine would not be able to fuzz test any protocol that requires sending more than one data set; some exceptions may occur if you can do what is sometimes referred to as session fixation. Any follow-up data set would be disregarded by the protocol's parser, as it would lack the required data to be valid.

State machines can also be used to test the logic of the protocol's parser where the state is "shuffled" so that, for example, the authentication process occurs after the request to download a file, or the authentication process is done more than once or even in reverse order—sending the password field before sending the user field.

These kinds of testing would fall under the category of logic test, and would be considered by many as not the classic fuzz testing. However, testing this is important, and many vulnerabilities have been discovered in relation to this kind of testing.

Summarize

To summarize, we would need the following:

1. An initial data set
2. Understand what it contains
3. Modify the value it contains
4. Provide that data to the protocol
5. If we later discover that a problem has occurred, be able to recreate the preceding "recipe"; if nothing happened, repeat step 1.

Down to Business

Up until now, we were talking about what is needed; from this point, we will be talking about how we do it.

Our coding language of choice is Perl, even though we believe you could build a fuzzer with any language, even Bash—of course, some languages would make it harder for you to build than others. We will take the file fuzzing example and use it; we will not be building a full-blown generic fuzzer, but more of a proof of concept fuzzer that is able to generate malformed BMP files.

We start by building a Perl Module (PM file) that will generate upon request a malformed value; for simplicity, it will not fuzz existing data, but will return one from the predefined list.

```
# Beyond Security Inc.
# Copyright 2007 - Noam Rathaus
package Generator;
my @MalformedValues = (
  "RepeatedAx1" =>    "A",    "RepeatedAx2" =>      "A"x2,
  "RepeatedAx4" =>    "A"x4,  "RepeatedAx8" =>      "A"x8,
  "RepeatedAx16" =>   "A"x16, "RepeatedAx32" =>     "A"x32,
  "RepeatedAx64" =>   "A"x64, "RepeatedAx128" =>    "A"x128,
  "RepeatedAx256" =>  "A"x256,       "RepeatedAx512" =>    "A"x512,
```

```perl
  "RepeatedAx1024" => "A"x1024,      "RepeatedAx2048" =>  "A"x2048,
  "RepeatedAx4096" => "A"x4096,      "RepeatedAx8192" =>  "A"x8192,
  "RepeatedAx16384" =>        "A"x16384,    "RepeatedAx32768" => "A"x32768,
  "RepeatedAx65536" =>        "A"x65536,
  "RepeatedNULLx1" => "\x00","RepeatedNULLx2" =>  "\x00"x2,
  "RepeatedNULLx4" => "\x00"x4,      "RepeatedNULLx8" =>  "\x00"x8,
  "RepeatedNULLx16" =>        "\x00"x16,    "RepeatedNULLx32" => "\x00"x32,
  "RepeatedNULLx64" =>        "\x00"x64,    "RepeatedNULLx128" =>"\x00"x128,
  "RepeatedNULLx256" =>        "\x00"x256,    "RepeatedNULLx512" =>"\x00"x512,
  "RepeatedNULLx1024" =>        "\x00"x1024,  "RepeatedNULLx2048" =>        "\x00"x2048,
  "RepeatedNULLx4096" =>        "\x00"x4096,  "RepeatedNULLx8192" =>        "\x00"x8192,
  "RepeatedNULLx16384" =>        "\x00"x16384, "RepeatedNULLx32768" =>        "\x00"x32768,
  "RepeatedNULLx65536" =>        "\x00"x65536,
  "Numeric -1" =>        "-1",  "Numeric -2" =>        "-2",
  "Numeric 0" =>        "0",
  "Binary -1 (BYTE)" =>        "\xFF", "Binary -2 (BYTE)" =>        "\xFE",
  "Binary 0 (BYTE)" =>        "\x00",
  "Binary -1 (2 BYTES)" =>  "\xFF\xFF", "Binary -2 (2 BYTES)" =>        "\xFF\xFE",
  "Binary 0 (2 BYTES)" =>   "\x00\x00",
  "Binary -2 (2 BYTES Reverse)" => "\xFE\xFF",
  "Binary -1 (3 BYTES)" =>  "\xFF\xFF\xFF", "Binary -2 (3 BYTES)" =>
"\xFF\xFF\xFE",
  "Binary 0 (3 BYTES)" =>   "\x00\x00\x00",
  "Binary -2 (3 BYTES Reverse)" => "\xFE\xFF\xFF",
  "Binary -1 (4 BYTES)" =>   "\xFF\xFF\xFF\xFF", "Binary -2 (4 BYTES)" =>
"\xFF\xFF\xFF\xFE",
  "Binary 0 (4 BYTES)" =>   "\x00\x00\x00\x00",
  "Binary -2 (4 BYTES Reverse)" => "\xFE\xFF\xFF\xFF",
  "Format String %sx1" => "%s"x1, "Format String %sx2" => "%s"x2,
  "Format String %sx4" => "%s"x4, "Format String %sx8" => "%s"x8,
  "Format String %sx16" => "%s"x16, "Format String %sx32" => "%s"x32,
  "Format String %xx1" => "%x"x1, "Format String %xx2" => "%x"x2,
  "Format String %xx4" => "%x"x4, "Format String %xx8" => "%x"x8,
  "Format String %xx16" => "%x"x16, "Format String %xx32" => "%x"x32,
  );
#use Data::Dumper;
#print Dumper(\@MalformedValues);
sub new {
  my $class = shift;
  my $self = bless(
```

```
  {
  'Main' => @_ ? shift : undef,
  },
  $class);
  return($self);
}
sub returnCount {
  my $class = shift;
  return scalar(@MalformedValues) / 2;
}
sub returnValueAt {
  my $class = shift;
  my $pos = shift;
  return $MalformedValues[$pos*2+1];
}
sub returnNameAt {
  my $class = shift;
  my $pos = shift;
  return $MalformedValues[$pos*2];
}
1;
```

As you can see in the preceding module, the arsenal of malformed values is far from complete, but can be easily extended to have additional types of attacks and test additional cases.

The next stage is to build an infrastructure to allow us to explain to our fuzzer how the protocol is built. We will define for our protocol that its values are either a constant (don t fuzz this value), a buffer (fuzz this value), or a length (change this value in accordance to the data we are bounded to; if it grows, increase our value, if it diminishes, decrease our value).

A BMP file contains of the following data structures (www.fortunecity.com/skyscraper/windows/364/bmpffrmt.html):

```
BITMAPFILEHEADER          bmfh;
BITMAPINFOHEADER          bmih;
RGBQUAD                   aColors[];
BYTE                      aBitmapBits[];
```

Where the BITMAPFILEHEADER is defined as:

```
WORD bfType; // must always be set to 'BM' to declare that this is a .bmp-file.
DWORD bfSize; // specifies the size of the file in bytes.
WORD bfReserved1; // must always be set to zero.
```

```
WORD bfReserved2; // must always be set to zero.
DWORD bfOffBits; // specifies the offset from the beginning of the file
to the bitmap data.
```

And BITMAPINFOHEADER is defined as:

```
DWORD biSize; // specifies the size of the BITMAPINFOHEADER structure, in bytes.
DWORD biWidth; // specifies the width of the image, in pixels.
DWORD biHeight; // specifies the height of the image, in pixels.
WORD biPlanes; // specifies the number of planes of the target device, must be
set to one.
WORD biBitCount; // specifies the number of bits per pixel.
DWORD biCompression; // Specifies the type of compression, usually set to zero
(no compression).
DWORD biSizeImage; // specifies the size of the image data, in bytes. If there is
no compression, it is valid to set this member to zero.
DWORD biXPelsPerMeter; // specifies the horizontal pixels per meter on the
designated target device, usually set to zero.
DWORD biYPelsPerMeter; // specifies the vertical pixels per meter on the
designated target device, usually set to zero.
DWORD biClrUsed; // specifies the number of colors used in the bitmap, if set to
zero the number of colors is calculated using the biBitCount member.
DWORD biClrImportant; // specifies the number of color that are 'important' for
the bitmap, if set to zero, all colors are important.
Followed by the RGBQUAD array:
BYTE rgbBlue; // specifies the blue part of the color.
BYTE rgbGreen; // specifies the green part of the color.
BYTE rgbRed; // specifies the red part of the color.
BYTE rgbReserved; // must always be set to zero.
```

Last but not least, the image data itself.

So, what would be the best method of representing the preceding data? A structured variable that defines four types of elements:

- Constants
- Buffers
- Length
- Structure

Constants are elements whose value does not change, buffers are elements we want to fuzz around with, Length are elements that contain the size value of another element, and structure is an element that contains other elements (in a nesting manner).

The following is the representation of the previous specification of the BMP file:

```
# Beyond Security Inc.
# Copyright 2007 - Noam Rathaus
package Protocol;
my @BMPStructure =
  (
    {
      "Name" => "bmfh",
      "Type" => "S",
      "Structure" =>
        [
          {
            "Name" => "bfType",
            "Type" => "C",
            "Default" => "BM",
          },
          {
            "Name" => "bfSize",
            "Type" => "L",
            "Bounded to" => "Size of File",
            "Size" => 4,
            "Order" => "Reverse",
          },
          {
            "Name" => "bfReserved1",
            "Type" => "C",
            "Default" => "\x00\x00",
          },
          {
            "Name" => "bfReserved2",
            "Type" => "C",
            "Default" => "\x00\x00",
          },
          {
            "Name" => "bfOffBits",
            "Type" => "C",
       "Default" => "\x36\x00\x00\x00"
          }
        ],
    },
```

```
{
  "Name" => "bmih",
  "Type" => "S",
    "Structure" =>
    [
      {
        "Name" => "biSize",
          "Type" => "C",
          "Default" => "\x28\x00\x00\x00",
        },
      {
        "Name" => "biWidth",
          "Type" => "B",
          "Default" => "\x10\x00\x00\x00",
          "Size" => 4,
        },
      {
        "Name" => "biHeight",
          "Type" => "B",
          "Default" => "\x10\x00\x00\x00",
          "Size" => 4,
        },
      {
        "Name" => "biPlanes",
          "Type" => "B",
          "Default" => "\x01\x00",
          "Size" => 2,
        },
      {
        "Name" => "biBitCount",
          "Type" => "B",
          "Default" => "\x08\x00",
          "Size" => 2,
        },
      {
        "Name" => "biCompression",
          "Type" => "C",
          "Default" => "\x00\x00\x00\x00",
        },
```

```
        {
       "Name" => "biSizeImage",
          "Type" => "B",
          "Default" => "\x36\x00\x00\x00",
          "Size" => 4,
         },
        {
       "Name" => "biXPelsPerMeter",
          "Type" => "B",
          "Default" => "\x00\x00\x00\x00",
          "Size" => 4,
         },
        {
       "Name" => "biYPelsPerMeter",
          "Type" => "B",
          "Default" => "\x00\x00\x00\x00",
          "Size" => 4,
         },
        {
       "Name" => "biClrUsed",
          "Type" => "B",
          "Default" => "\x00\x00\x00\x00",
          "Size" => 4,
         },
        {
       "Name" => "biClrImportant",
          "Type" => "B",
          "Default" => "\x00\x00\x00\x00",
          "Size" => 4,
         },
     ],
   },
 {
  "Name" => "aColors",
     "Type" => "B",
     "Default" => "\xFF\x20",
     },
 {
  "Name" => "aBitmapBits",
    "Type" => "B",
```

```
      "Default" =>
"\x01\x10\x20\x30\x40\x50\x60\x7F\x8F\x9F\xAF\xBF\xCF\xDF\xFF".
"\x02\x10\x20\x30\x40\x50\x60\x7F\x8F\x9F\xAF\xBF\xCF\xDF\xFF".
"\x03\x10\x20\x30\x40\x50\x60\x7F\x8F\x9F\xAF\xBF\xCF\xDF\xFF".
"\x04\x10\x20\x30\x40\x50\x60\x7F\x8F\x9F\xAF\xBF\xCF\xDF\xFF".
"\x05\x10\x20\x30\x40\x50\x60\x7F\x8F\x9F\xAF\xBF\xCF\xDF\xFF".
"\x06\x10\x20\x30\x40\x50\x60\x7F\x8F\x9F\xAF\xBF\xCF\xDF\xFF".
"\x07\x10\x20\x30\x40\x50\x60\x7F\x8F\x9F\xAF\xBF\xCF\xDF\xFF".
"\x08\x10\x20\x30\x40\x50\x60\x7F\x8F\x9F\xAF\xBF\xCF\xDF\xFF".
"\x09\x10\x20\x30\x40\x50\x60\x7F\x8F\x9F\xAF\xBF\xCF\xDF\xFF".
"\x0A\x10\x20\x30\x40\x50\x60\x7F\x8F\x9F\xAF\xBF\xCF\xDF\xFF".
"\x0B\x10\x20\x30\x40\x50\x60\x7F\x8F\x9F\xAF\xBF\xCF\xDF\xFF".
"\x0C\x10\x20\x30\x40\x50\x60\x7F\x8F\x9F\xAF\xBF\xCF\xDF\xFF".
"\x0D\x10\x20\x30\x40\x50\x60\x7F\x8F\x9F\xAF\xBF\xCF\xDF\xFF".
"\x0E\x10\x20\x30\x40\x50\x60\x7F\x8F\x9F\xAF\xBF\xCF\xDF\xFF".
"\x0F\x10\x20\x30\x40\x50\x60\x7F\x8F\x9F\xAF\xBF\xCF\xDF\xFF".
"\x0F\x10\x20\x30\x40\x50\x60\x7F\x8F\x9F\xAF\xBF\xCF\xDF\xFF".
"\x10\x10\x20\x30\x40\x50\x60\x7F\x8F\x9F\xAF\xBF\xCF\xDF\xFF"
      },
  );
sub new {
  my $class = shift;
  my $self = bless(
    {
      'Main' => @_ ? shift : undef,
    },
    $class);
  return($self);
}
sub returnStructure {
  my $class = shift;
  return (\@BMPStructure);
}
1;
```

Notice that we have written in several locations the Size attribute to allow our fuzzer to avoid sending data that is too small or too big to fit the field. This is important for protocols that have strict header structures, as sending a malformed (in size) header would likely get the parser of the structure to discard the data.

Now that we have a generator of data and a specification of the protocol, we need something to take them and combine them together—this is the Fuzzer.pl script:

```perl
#!/usr/bin/perl
# Beyond Security Inc.
# Copyright 2007 - Noam Rathaus
use strict;
use Protocol;
use Generator;
my $refProtocol = new Protocol;
my $refGenerator = new Generator;
my $CombinationCount = $refGenerator->returnCount();
print "Test cases: $CombinationCount\n";
#use Data::Dumper;
#print Dumper($refProtocol->returnStructure());
my %GlobalPositions;
my @GlobalProtocol = @{$refProtocol->returnStructure()};
my $Counter = 0;
while (1 == incrementPos(\@GlobalProtocol))
{
  $Counter++;
my @Data;
@Data = generateProtocol(\@GlobalProtocol, \@Data);
my $data = "";
my $lastWord = "";
my $preData = join("", @Data);
foreach my $dataElement (@Data)
{
  if (substr($dataElement, 0, 3) eq "\$SZ")
  {
    #print "dataElement: $dataElement\n";
    my $Size = substr($dataElement, 3, 1);
    my $Length = length($preData);
    #print "Length: $Length\n";
    $dataElement = pack("L1", $Length);
    #printf ("dataElement: %x\n", $dataElement);
  }
  $data .= $dataElement;
}
open(FILE, "> /tmp/data$Counter.bmp");
```

```perl
print FILE $data;
  close(FILE);
};
## This function finds the first suitable place and moves its position by one
sub incrementPos
{
 my $ptrProtocol = shift;
 my @Protocol;
 if (defined $ptrProtocol)
 {
 @Protocol = @{$ptrProtocol};
 }
 foreach my $ptrElement (@Protocol)
 {
   my %Element;
   if (defined $ptrElement)
   {
     %Element = %{$ptrElement};
   }
   if (%Element->{"Type"} eq "L")
   {
     next;
   }
   elsif (%Element->{"Type"} eq "C")
   {
     next;
   }
   elsif (%Element->{"Type"} eq "S")
   {
     my @Structure;
     if (defined %Element->{"Structure"})
     {
       @Structure = @{%Element->{"Structure"}};
     }
     my $ret = incrementPos(\@Structure);
     if ($ret == 1)
     {
       return 1;
     }
   }
```

```perl
    elsif (%Element->{"Type"} eq "B")
  {
    my $Pos = undef;
    if (defined %GlobalPositions->{%Element->{'Name'}})
    {
      $Pos = %GlobalPositions->{%Element->{'Name'}};
    }
        if ($Pos != -1)
        {
          if (not defined $Pos)
          {
            $Pos = 0;
          }
          else
          {
            $Pos++;
          }
          if (defined %Element->{'Size'} and %Element->{'Size'} > 0)
          {
            #printf ("Size requirement: %d\n", %Element->{'Size'});
            while ($Pos <= $CombinationCount && length($refGenerator->
returnValueAt($Pos)) != %Element->{'Size'})
            {
              $Pos ++;
            }
          }
        if ($Pos >= $CombinationCount)
        {
          %GlobalPositions->{%Element->{'Name'}} = -1;
        }
        else
        {
          %GlobalPositions->{%Element->{'Name'}} = $Pos;
        return 1;
      }
    }
  }
  }
  return 0;
}
```

```perl
sub generateProtocol
{
 my $ptrProtocol = shift;
 my $ptrData = shift;
 my @Data;
 if (defined $ptrData)
 {
   @Data = @{$ptrData};
 }
 my @Protocol;
 if (defined $ptrProtocol)
 {
   @Protocol = @{$ptrProtocol};
 }
 foreach my $ptrElement (@Protocol)
 {
   my %Element;
   if (defined $ptrElement)
   {
     %Element = %{$ptrElement};
   }
   #print "Handling: ".%Element->{'Name'}."\n";
   if(%Element->{"Type"} eq "B")
   {
     my $Value;
     if (not defined %GlobalPositions->{%Element->{'Name'}} or -1 ==
(%GlobalPositions->{%Element->{'Name'}}))
     {
       #print "Don't Fuzz ".%Element->{'Name'}."\n";
       $Value = %Element->{"Default"};
     }
     else
     {
       $Value = $refGenerator->returnValueAt(%GlobalPositions->{%Element-> {'Name'}});
       if (defined %Element->{"Size"} and length($Value) != %Element->{"Size"})
       {
         $Value = %Element->{"Default"};
       } else
       {
       print "Fuzzing data ".%Element->{"Name"}.
```

```
        " with ". $refGenerator->returnNameAt(%GlobalPositions->{%Element->
{'Name'}}).
        " (".%GlobalPositions->{%Element->{'Name'}}.")\n";
    }
  }
  push(@Data, $Value);
}
elsif (%Element->{"Type"} eq "C")
{
  # Just send it
  push(@Data, %Element->{"Default"});
  }
  elsif (%Element->{"Type"} eq "L")
  {
    # What is the size of the element?
    if (%Element->{"Bounded to"} eq "Size of File")
    {
    # We need to wait for the file to be generated before filling this in lets
push the reserved $FILESIZE inside
    my $Size = %Element->{"Size"};
      push(@Data, "\$SZ$Size");
    }
  }
  elsif (%Element->{"Type"} eq "S")
  {
    # Recursive go
    my @Structure;
    if (defined %Element->{"Structure"})
    {
      @Structure = @{%Element->{"Structure"}};
    }
    @Data = generateProtocol(\@Structure, \@Data);
  }
  else {
    die("Undefined: ".%Element->{"Type"}."\n");
  }
}
  return @Data;
}
```

Running the above Fuzzer.pl script, will generate 204 test cases as we are skipping on cases that don't match our Buffer's size requirements. This is of course a very simple fuzzer, but it is good for a few things:

- Easily extend the malformed values list
- Use the same Fuzzer for different file types – the Protocol structure is not limited to BMP files
- The Fuzzer understand a few basic attributes such as Size and Data Length
- Fuzzer's code can be used to also automate the process of testing the generated data with your program

Simplest Fuzz Testing Find Issues

We just completed your very first fuzzer; more specifically, your very own BMP file fuzzer. In most cases, you would probably wonder what such a simple fuzzer could do. Well, you won't believe it but Kuickshow (KDE image/slideshow viewer) version 4:3.5.7-2 is actually vulnerable to one of the BMP files generated by the previous fuzzer.

The vulnerability isn't an exploitable buffer overflow; rather, it appears to be a form of a DoS where the BMP parser appears to enter an endless loop. If you copied the previous code exactly, data28.bmp is the culprit that causes the endless loop.

The malformed content of the BMP file is:

```
0000000000 42 4d 37 01 00 00 00 00 00 00 36 00 00 00 28 00  BM7......6...(.
0000000016 00 00 10 00 00 00 10 00 00 00 01 00 00 00 00 00  ..............
0000000032 00 00 36 00 00 00 00 00 00 00 00 00 00 00 00 00  ..6...........
0000000048 00 00 00 00 00 00 ff 20 01 10 20 30 40 50 60 7f  ......ÿ .. 0@P`.
0000000064 8f 9f af bf cf df ff 02 10 20 30 40 50 60 7f 8f  ..¯¿Ïßÿ.. 0@P`..
0000000080 9f af bf cf df ff 03 10 20 30 40 50 60 7f 8f 9f  .¯¿Ïßÿ.. 0@P`...
0000000096 af bf cf df ff 04 10 20 30 40 50 60 7f 8f 9f af  ¯¿Ïßÿ.. 0@P`...¯
0000000112 bf cf df ff 05 10 20 30 40 50 60 7f 8f 9f af bf  ¿Ïßÿ.. 0@P`...¯¿
0000000128 cf df ff 06 10 20 30 40 50 60 7f 8f 9f af bf cf  Ïßÿ.. 0@P`...¯¿Ï
0000000144 df ff 07 10 20 30 40 50 60 7f 8f 9f af bf cf df  ßÿ.. 0@P`...¯¿Ïß
0000000160 ff 08 10 20 30 40 50 60 7f 8f 9f af bf cf df ff  ÿ.. 0@P`...¯¿Ïßÿ
0000000176 09 10 20 30 40 50 60 7f 8f 9f af bf cf df ff 0a  .. 0@P`...¯¿Ïßÿ.
0000000192 10 20 30 40 50 60 7f 8f 9f af bf cf df ff 0b 10  . 0@P`...¯¿Ïßÿ..
0000000208 20 30 40 50 60 7f 8f 9f af bf cf df ff 0c 10 20   0@P`...¯¿Ïßÿ..
0000000224 30 40 50 60 7f 8f 9f af bf cf df ff 0d 10 20 30  0@P`...¯¿Ïßÿ.. 0
```

```
0000000240 40 50 60 7f 8f 9f af bf cf df ff 0e 10 20 30 40  @P`,...¯¿Ïßÿ.. 0@
0000000256 50 60 7f 8f 9f af bf cf df ff 0f 10 20 30 40 50  P`,...¯¿Ïßÿ.. 0@P
0000000272 60 7f 8f 9f af bf cf df ff 0f 10 20 30 40 50 60  `...¯¿Ïßÿ.. 0@P`
0000000288 7f 8f 9f af bf cf df ff 10 10 20 30 40 50 60 7f  ...¯¿Ïßÿ.. 0@P`.
0000000304 8f 9f af bf cf df ff                             ..¯¿Ïßÿ
```

For easier reading, we have marked the fields either with or without an underline in an interlaced method, and in bold the malformed value. The malformed value of 0x0000 for the BPP (biBitCount) field means that the file has no bits count. This causes an endless loop, as the code does not know how much to move forward when it reads the data section of the image.

```
Going through the code found in Imlib/load.c you would notice:
  bpp = (int)word;
    if (bpp != 1 && bpp != 4 && bpp != 8 && bpp && 16 && bpp != 24 && bpp != 32)
      {
        fprintf(stderr, "IMLIB ERROR: unknown bitdepth in file\n");
        return NULL;
      }
```

At first glance, it looks like a value of 0x0000 shouldn't have passed, but at closer inspection you'll notice && bpp &&, which means that the value of 0x0000 will not enter into the check, but rather into the loop that reads the data from the file.

The source goes like so; at line 784 you have the following test:

```
if (bpp < 16)
```

And since inside we have only the following tests, and nothing else, the code will never increment the value of column, and the loop will never terminate.

```
if (bpp == 1)
{
..
}
else if (bpp == 4)
{
..
}
else if (bpp == 8)
{
..
}
```

Congratulations! You just found your very first vulnerability using a file fuzzer.

You're probably wondering what's next. Did you find everything? Has the fuzzer found every possible bug in the program? Well, it didn't. There are at least two other issues we know of in the _LoadBMP function that cause the library to read past the end of file or write to memory that hasn't been allocated, which both in turn cause it to crash.

NOTE

For those worried about full disclosure, we reported the issues in LoadBMP several months ago to the Debian security group; they have not been addressed.

## Chapter 7

Integration of Fuzzing in the Development Cycle

Solutions in this chapter:

- **Why Is Fuzzing Important to Include in a Software Development Cycle?**

- **Setting Expectations for Fuzzers in a Software Development Lifecycle**

- **Setting the Plan for Implementing Fuzzers into a Software Development Lifecycle**

- **Understanding How to Increase the Effectiveness of Fuzzers, and Avoiding Any Big Gotchas**

☑ **Summary**

☑ **Solutions Fast Track**

☑ **Frequently Asked Questions**

Introduction

Throughout this book, you've seen time after time where bugs were easily found via fuzzing. In many cases, these bugs could have easily been found by software vendors prior to releasing their software with a little bit of due diligence. This chapter is written from the perspective of how vendors would go about integrating fuzzing into their software development lifecycle.

First, fuzzing needs to be a subset of an overall security plan. Two of the more prominent software security development processes are "The Security Development Lifecycle" from Microsoft (www.microsoft.com/mspress/books/8753.aspx), and "Comprehensive, Lightweight Application Security Process," or CLASP (www.owasp.org/index.php/Category:OWASP_CLASP_Project), sponsored by the Open Web Application Security Project (OWASP). Using either of these processes will help in getting your security effort off on the right foot. Fuzzing simply fits into these broader plans as a component of more robust security testing.

The popularity of fuzzing among security researchers, large corporate customers, and those with malicious intent is growing rapidly. Not performing fuzz testing on your software will leave you open to others finding these software flaws for you. Anyone who has had to respond to externally found and publicly known security vulnerability knows this is not a good thing. The Month of Browser Bugs (MoBB http://browserfun.blogspot.com/) was eye opening to many as to the number of flaws that could be found via fuzzing. Those familiar with the complexity of the parsers involved with Internet browsers should not be too surprised that these types of bugs exist.

Some software vendors are already drinking the fuzzing Kool-Aid. Microsoft has publicly stated that fuzzing is a requirement for any product that ships as part of its Security Development Lifecycle (SDL). A number of other companies have been putting similar requirements on their software.

Our hope is that software vendors can use this book to help produce more secure and more reliable software. They'll look at fuzzers as being complementary to their security testing currently in place, and open up more time for software vendors to do more in-depth testing, as the fuzzers will allow for automation of some of the more mundane security testing tasks. Included in this is the realization of what types of flaws fuzzers are good at finding and those that are better left to manual testing.

Why Is Fuzzing Important to Include in a Software Development Cycle?

If your company develops software or services, one of the first questions you should ask is, "why should I run fuzzers?" The answer to that, touched on in earlier chapters, should be straightforward.

- Put simply, fuzzers are effective at finding bugs.

- Fuzzers save time and are cheap alternatives to manual security testing.

- External security researchers and malicious individuals will run them for you if you do not.

In other words, fuzzers reduce test costs, find bugs, and help in preventing folks outside your organization from finding embarrassing flaws in your software. Sign me up! So, if your product is actively taking user input from outside sources, the question really isn't "should I run a fuzzer," but "how do I get started?"

Before we jump into how to integrate and implement fuzzing into your development cycle, we'll dig deeper into why fuzzers are important to run.

Security Testing Workload

For anyone who has ever worked in Quality Assurance, it should be obvious that you are always resource and time constrained. That given with the old test adage, "you can only prove the existence of bugs, but not the absence of them," are two particular reasons why performing security testing can be difficult. The test team has a long grocery list of types of tests to run, including, but not limited to:

- Unit testing
- Integration testing
- Scenario testing
- Functionality testing
- Reliability testing
- Performance testing

- Accessibility testing
- Testability analysis
- Usability testing
- Internationalization testing
- Localization testing
- Security testing

All this testing requires a significant amount of time. Any test team worth its salt focuses a good amount of energy on automating what testing it can. Performing all testing manually and repeating every release (in some cases multiple times a release) is very time consuming and inefficient.

NOTE

We'll be referring to the test team (and tester) frequently, but being time and resource constrained applies even more so in smaller organizations where the development team owns the testing of the software or where the testing team is substantially outnumbered by developers.

Security testing is hard for most testers (and from our experience, even more difficult for the average developer). It is extremely time consuming, requires the test team to think in unfamiliar ways, and forces some to focus on technical details they are not necessarily accustomed to. Additionally, at times there seems to be an unlimited number of security test cases that could be run. To stress our point on the time it takes to do security testing, we'll construct a simple example file that is read in by an application. This file is a Rich Text Format file saved out by Microsoft Word 2003 and contains four things mixed in with regular black Times New Roman size 12 font text: red and enlarged text, a link, and a small image as seen in Figure 7.1.

NOTE

Rich Text Format (RTF) is a proprietary file format created by Microsoft in the late 1980s generally used by word processors.

Figure 7.1 Simple RTF Document Consumed by Microsoft Word

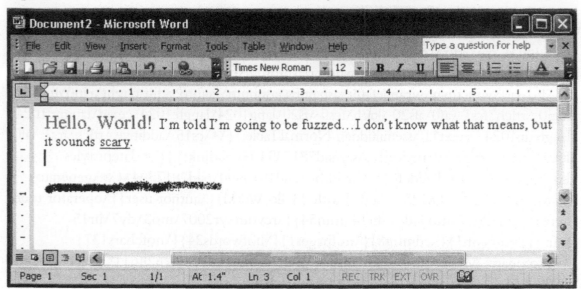

Here is the entire RTF document:

{\rtf1\adeflang1025\ansi\ansicpg1252\uc1\adeff0\deff0\stshfdbch0\stshfloch0
\stshfhich0\stshfbi0\deflang1033\deflangfe1033{\fonttbl{\f0\froman\fcharset0
\fprq2{*\panose 02020603050405020304}Times New Roman;}{\f122\froman
\fcharset238\fprq2 Times New Roman CE;}{\f123\froman\fcharset204\fprq2
Times New Roman Cyr;}

{\f125\froman\fcharset161\fprq2 Times New Roman Greek;}{\f126\froman
\fcharset162\fprq2 Times New Roman Tur;}{\f127\fbidi \froman\fcharset177\fprq2
Times New Roman (Hebrew);}{\f128\fbidi \froman\fcharset178\fprq2 Times New
Roman (Arabic);}

{\f129\froman\fcharset186\fprq2 Times New Roman Baltic;}{\f130\froman
\fcharset163\fprq2 Times New Roman (Vietnamese);}}{\colortbl;\red0\green0
\ blue0;\red0\green0\blue255;\red0\green255\blue255;\red0\green255\blue0;
\ red255\green0\blue255;

\red255\green0\blue0;\red255\green255\blue0;\red255\green255\blue255;\ red0
\green0\blue128;\red0\green128\blue128;\red0\green128\blue0;\red128\green0
\b lue128;\red128\green0\blue0;\red128\green128\blue0;\red128\green128
\blue128;\ red192\green192\blue192;}

{\stylesheet{\ql \li0\ri0\widctlpar\wrapdefault\aspalpha\aspnum\faauto\adjustright
\rin0\lin0\itap0 \rtlch\fcs1 \af0\afs24\alang1025 \ltrch\fcs0 \fs24\lang1033

\langfe1033\cgrid\langnp1033\langfenp1033 \snext0 Normal;}{*\cs10
\ additive \ssemihidden

Default Paragraph Font;}{*\ts11\tsrowd\trftsWidthB3\trpaddl108\trpaddr108
\trpaddfl3\ trpaddft3\trpaddfb3\trpaddfr3\tblind0\tblindtype3\tscellwidthfts0
\tsvertalt\tsbrdrt\ tsbrdrl\tsbrdrb\tsbrdrr\tsbrdrdgl\tsbrdrdgr\tsbrdrh\tsbrdrv
\ql \li0\ri0\widctlpar\wrapdefault\aspalpha\aspnum\faauto\adjustright\rin0\lin0
\itap0 \rtlch\fcs1 \af0\afs20 \ltrch\fcs0 \fs20\lang1024\langfe1024\cgrid\langnp1024
\langfenp1024 \snext11 \ssemihidden NormalTable;}{*\cs15 \additive \rtlch\fcs1 \af0
\ltrch\fcs0 \ul\cf2 \sbasedon10 \styrsid7817394 Hyperlink;}}{*\latentstyles
\lsdstimax156\lsdlockeddef0}{*\rsidtbl \rsid1910890\rsid7817394}{*\generator
Microsoft Word 11.0.8125;}{\info{\title Hello, World}{\author user}{\operator user}
{\creatim\yr2007\mo3\dy7\hr14\min54}{\revtim\yr2007\mo3\dy7\hr15
\min4}{\version1}{\edmins8}{\nofpages1}{\nofwords24}{\nofchars137}
{*\company Microsoft Corporation}{\nofcharsws160}{\vern24611}{*\password
00000000} }{*\xmlnstbl {\xmlns1 http://schemas.mic
rosoft.com/office/word/2003/wordml} }\paperw12240\paperh15840\margl1800
\ margr1800\margt1440\margb1440\gutter0\ltrsect
\widowctrl\ftnbj\aenddoc\donotembedsysfont1\donotembedlingdata0\grfdoc
events0\validatexml1\showplaceholdtext0\ignoremixedcontent0\saveinvalidxml0
\showxmlerrors1\noxlattoyen\expshrtn\noultrlspc\dntblnsbdb\nospaceforul
\formshade\horzdoc\dgmargin\dghspace180
\dgvspace180\dghorigin1800\dgvorigin1440\dghshow1\dgvshow1
\jexpand\viewkind1\viewscale100\pgbrdrhead\pgbrdrfoot\splytwnine\ftnlytwnine
\htmautsp\ nolnhtadjtbl\useltbaln\alntblind\ lytcalctblwd\ lyttblrtgr\lnbrkrule
\ nobrkwrptbl\viewnobound1\snaptogridincell\allowfieldendsel
\wrppunct\asianbrkrule\rsidroot7817394\newtblstyruls\nogrowautofit \fet0
{*\wgrffmtfilter 013f}\ilfomacatclnup0\ltrpar \sectd \ltrsect\linex0\endnhere
\sectlinegrid360\sectdefaultcl\sftnbj {*\pnseclvl1\pnucrm\pnstart1\pnindent720
\pnhang {\pntxta .} }
{*\pnseclvl2\pnucltr\pnstart1\pnindent720\pnhang {\pntxta .} }{*\pnseclvl3
\pndec\pnstart1\pnindent720\pnhang {\pntxta .} }{*\pnseclvl4\pnlcltr\pnstart1
\pnindent720\pnhang {\pntxta)} }{*\pnseclvl5\pndec\pnstart1\pnindent720
\pnhang {\pntxtb (}{\pntxta)} }
{*\pnseclvl6\pnlcltr\pnstart1\pnindent720\pnhang {\pntxtb (}{\pntxta)} }{*
\pnseclvl7\pnlcrm\pnstart1\pnindent720\pnhang {\pntxtb (}{\pntxta)} }{*\pnseclvl8
\pnlcltr\pnstart1\pnindent720\pnhang {\pntxtb (}{\pntxta)} }{*\pnseclvl9

```
\pnlcrm\pnstart1\pnindent720\pnhang {\pntxtb (}{\pntxta )} }\pard\plain \ltrpar
\ql \li0\ri0\widctlpar\wrapdefault\aspalpha\aspnum\faauto\adjustright\rin0\lin0
\itap0 \rtlch\fcs1 \af0\afs24\alang1025 \ltrch\fcs0
\fs24\lang1033\langfe1033\cgrid\langnp1033\langfenp1033 {\rtlch\fcs1 \af0
\afs32 \ltrch\fcs0 \fs32\cf6\insrsid7817394\charrsid7817394 Hello, World!}{\rtlch
\fcs1 \af0 \ltrch\fcs0 \insrsid7817394 I\rquote m told I\rquote m going to be
fuzzed\'85I don
\rquote t know what that means, but it sounds }{\field{\*\fldinst {\rtlch\fcs1 \af0
\ltrch\fcs0 \insrsid7817394 HYPERLINK "http://www.youtube.com/watch?v=2T5_
0AGdFic" }{\rtlch\fcs1 \af0 \ltrch\fcs0 \insrsid1910890 {\*\datafield
00d0c9ea79f9bace118c8200aa004ba90b0200000003000000e0c9ea79f9bace118c8200a
a004ba90b560000006800740074007000 3a002f002f007700770077002e0079006f0075
0074007500620065002e0063006f006d002f0077007006100074006300680 03f0076003d00
3200540035005f00300041004700640046006900
63000000}}}{\fldrslt {\rtlch\fcs1 \af0 \ltrch\fcs0 \cs15\ul\cf2\insrsid7817394
\charrsid7817394 scary}}}\sectd \linex0\endnhere\sectlinegrid360\sectdefaultcl
\sftnbj {\rtlch\fcs1 \af0 \ltrch\fcs0 \insrsid7817394 .
\par
\par }{\rtlch\fcs1 \af0 \ltrch\fcs0 \insrsid7817394 {\pict{\*\picprop\shplid1025
{\sp{\sn shapeType}{\sv 75} }{\sp{\sn fFlipH}{\sv 0} }{\sp{\sn fFlipV}{\sv 0} }
{\sp{\sn pibFlags}{\sv 2} }{\sp{\sn fLine}{\sv 0} }{\sp{\sn fLayoutInCell}{\sv 1} } }
\picscalex100\picscaley100\piccropl0\piccropr0\piccropt0\piccropb0\picw4551
\pich1296\picwgoal2580\pichgoal735\wmetafile8\bliptag229526163\blipupi-96
{\*\blipuid 0dae4a93ba6c7d9fabce1327556fdbe9}
010009000003960200000000710200000000040000000301080005000000b0200000
000050000000c023200ad00030000001e000400000007010400710200 00
410b2000cc003100ac00000000003100ac00000000002800000 0ac0000003100000001
0001000000000000000000000000000000000000000000000000000000
0000ffffff00ffffffffffffffffffffffffffffffffffff00101ffffffffffffffffffffffffffffffffffff00101
ffffffffffffffffffff
ffffffffffffffffffffff00101ffffffffffffffffffffffffffffffffffff00101ffffffffffffffffffffffffffff
ffffff00101ffff
ffffffffffffffffffffff00101ffffffffffffffffffffffffffffffffffff00101ffffffffffffffffffffffffffffffff
ffffffffffff
ffffffff00101ffffffffffffffffffffffffffffffffffff00101ffffffffffffffffffffffffffffffffffff00101fff
ffffffffffffffffff
```

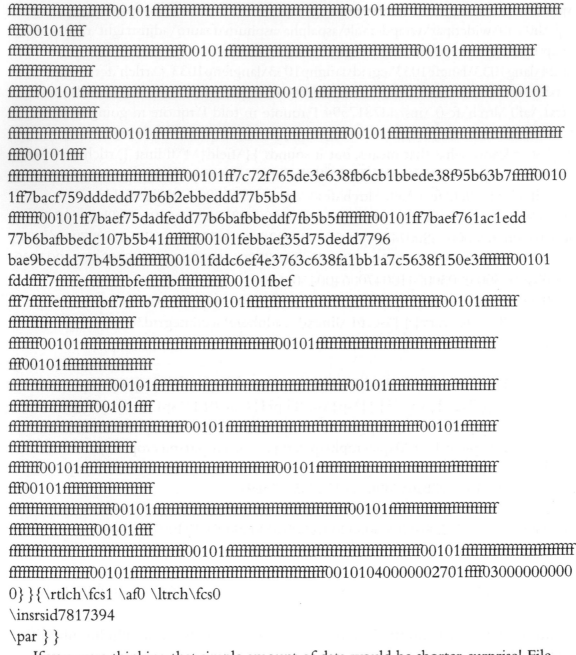

```
 fffffffffffffffffffffffff00101ffffffffffffffffffffffffffffffffffffffffffff00101ffffffffffffffffffffffffffffffffffffffffffffff
ffff00101ffff
fffffffffffffffffffffffffffff00101ffffffffffffffffffffffffffffffffffffffffffff00101ffffffffffffffffffff
ffffffffffffffffffff
ffffff00101ffffffffffffffffffffffffffffffffffffffffffff00101ffffffffffffffffffffffffffffffffffffffffffffffff00101
ffffffffffffffffffff
ffffffffffffffffffffffff00101ffffffffffffffffffffffffffffffffffffffffffff00101ffffffffffffffffffffffffffffffffffffffffffffffff
ffff00101ffff
ffffffffffffffffffffffffffffffffffffffff00101ff7c72f765de3e638fb6cb1bbede38f95b63b7fffff0010
1ff7bacf759dddedd77b6b2ebbeddd77b5b5d
fffffff00101ff7baef75dadfedd77b6bafbbeddf7fb5b5ffffffff00101ff7baef761ac1edd
77b6bafbbedc107b5b41fffffff00101febbaef35d75dedd7796
bae9becdd77b4b5dfffffff00101fddc6ef4e3763c638fa1bb1a7c5638f150e3fffffff00101
fddffff7fffffeffffffffbfefffffbffffffffff00101fbef
fff7fffffeffffffffbff7ffffb7fffffffff00101ffffffffffffffffffffffffffffffffffffffffffff00101ffffffff
ffffffffffffffffffffffffffffff
fffffff00101ffffffffffffffffffffffffffffffffffffffffffff00101ffffffffffffffffffffffffffffffff
fff00101ffffffffffffffffffffff
ffffffffffffffffffffffff00101ffffffffffffffffffffffffffffffffffffffffffff00101ffffffffffffffffffffffff
ffffffffffffffffffff00101ffff
ffffffffffffffffffffffffffff00101ffffffffffffffffffffffffffffffffffffffffffff00101fffffff
ffffffffffffffffffffffffff
ffffff00101ffffffffffffffffffffffffffffffffffffffffffff00101ffffffffffffffffffffffffffffffff
fff00101ffffffffffffffffffffff
ffffffffffffffffffffffff00101ffffffffffffffffffffffffffffffffffffffffffff00101ffffffffffffffffffff
fffffffffffffffffff00101ffff
fffffffffffffffffffffffffffff00101fffffffffffffffffffffffffffffffffffffffffffff00101ffffffffffffffffffffffffffffffffffff
fffffffffffffffffffffff00101ffffffffffffffffffffffffffffffffffffffffffffff00101040000002701fffff03000000000
0}}{\rtlch\fcs1 \af0 \ltrch\fcs0
\insrsid7817394
\par }}
```

If you were thinking that simple amount of data would be shorter, surprise! File formats can be quite complex (and RTF is not even one of the more complex). In any case, if you're responsible for security testing the RTF format, you'll have your work cut out for you. Just in this simple file with a few bits of text and an image, you have several hundred inputs that will be parsed when the file is opened. The level of accessibility you have to the source code and the developer can significantly help decrease your testing cost because you'll understand how the inputs are parsed, which can be used to come up with more direct tests that can be equivalence classed. However, for this example, let's assume you don't have access to the developer or the source, but are ultimately accountable for the security of this file format.

What types of tests might we try on these different inputs? Here are a few ideas:

- Large strings (but, what size is best?)
- Integer manipulation (but, to what?)
- Character insertion (which characters?)
- Character deletion
- Deleted inputs
- Repeated inputs
- Altering input and character order
- Unique characters that have special meaning in the file format (such as curly braces or slashes in RTF)
- Control characters (such CR, LF, and NULL)
- Format string insertion

This list could be much longer, as it is simply a starting point for conversation. As we now have a list of 10 or so different types of test, we'll want to try them all. There are some obvious open questions still, such as when we're doing our buffer overrun testing, what length of string we should try, or who is responsible for parsing the embedded graphics file in our document. For now, we'll continue moving forward with our testing ignorant to those questions and simply say that for each test type we'll run two different tests for every input we'll be testing. So, these 10 types will produce 20 test cases for every input.

Manually security testing this format would require the tester to:

1. Open the file in a binary editor.
2. Alter one of the inputs using one of the test cases listed previously.
3. Save the file using the binary editor.

4. Open the file using the application associated with that file format.

5. Repeat steps 1 trough 4 for every test case on every input (or more appropriately, every piece of the document that is parsed out).

If we're fast, one test may take 30 seconds. For the sake of argument, let's say there are 500 inputs in this document. For each input, we'll try our 20 test cases. Doing the math:

        500   (fields to test)
         20   (number of tests to run on each input)
    ×   30   (seconds to run one test)
        300,000

It would take 300,000 seconds, or a little more than 83 hours, to manually test this small piece of the file format. That is 83 hours for partial test coverage. More comprehensive coverage on the full file format would take several work weeks longer. Moreover, this number does not include the time it takes to manually investigate potential issues you uncover.

NOTE

The preceding numbers do not take into account whether different inputs can be equivalence classed (or if certain tests don't apply—like integer manipulation on strings). In our experience, most testers have a difficult time determining exactly what can be equivalence classed and generally side on over-testing.

As you can see, this problem has "automate me" written all over it. A good file fuzzer can run through an order of magnitude of the number of cases just described. Just kick off the file fuzzer before you head out Friday evening, and when you get back to work on Monday morning, a good portion of your security testing will be done for you.

Doing fuzz testing on your software will significantly reduce the cost of security testing your application. With that said, do not expect fuzzers to magically find all the security flaws in your product.

Setting Expectations for Fuzzers in a Software Development Lifecycle

While fuzzers are certainly a great way to find bugs in many different applications, expectations should be set appropriately on their effectiveness. Having that knowledge will better equip you when integrating fuzzing into your development lifecycle.

Fuzzing as a Panacea

Hip hip hooray! Fuzzers have gotten a lot of press lately, with some folks saying that fuzzers can and will find all application flaws. Put simply, this is now and never will be true. Fuzzers will continue to find more types of flaws and will become better at choosing what tests to execute and when, but there is no way a fuzzer will find all the vulnerabilities in an application with a moderately sized attack surface.

What Fuzzers Won't Find

To expand on the topic of don't bet the farm that fuzzers will find everything, we'd like to share a few instances where fuzzers typically have a hard time. That's not to say they could never find these types of bugs, but most fuzzers today do not. Here's a small list of some typical bugs not found by fuzzers:

Logical flaws   We've never met a fuzzer that was able to find logical flaws on a given application without intervention on the part of the person running the fuzzer. Let's say you're testing some sort of session identifier issued by the server to the client and sent by the client in subsequent requests for the server to determine who you are. For a fuzzer to be effective at testing this feature, it would need to know that a) this parameter is a session identifier, b) understand how to test for session flaws, and c) understand when a bug is hit.

Design flaws   Most fuzzers do not understand the design of the application they are testing. If an application decides to write out private data with world read/write access to it, the fuzzer would likely not notice.

Parser-specific flaws   Each parser is different, and understanding the context of the parser is important. For example, an application may have a token replacement routine, and unless the fuzzer knew what tokens to send in, it would never hit that code path.

Second order injection flaws   Flaws the application does not hit initially; for example, a backend scheduled task that reads data every night at midnight and uses it to construct SQL queries that are susceptible to SQL injection.

Stateful bugs   It can be difficult to find and reproduce vulnerabilities where the application needs to be in a certain state or mode before the vulnerability presents itself.

New vulnerability types   Fuzzers are written by humans, and if a new vulnerability type exists tomorrow, fuzzers would need to be updated to attempt those tests.

Many of these flaws could be found, but they require a couple of things: a fuzzer that is smart enough to understand how to test for these types of flaws, and the ability to monitor if the attack succeeded. Both of these may be nontrivial depending on the fuzzer you use for your testing. Monitoring is an important concept in understanding your test coverage and is covered in more detail later in this chapter.

Fuzzer Effectiveness

You should consider fuzzers as a backstop for the rest of the security development lifecycle. When fuzzers are integrated with other tools such as threat modeling, static and runtime code analysis tools, security code reviews, and penetration testing, they all help to reduce the number of vulnerabilities found after software is released.

According to the book *The Security Development Lifecycle* by Michael Howard and Steve Lipner, "At Microsoft, about 20 to 25 percent of security bugs are found through fuzzing a product before it is shipped." This figure is easily believable, but it is worth pointing out a few things:

- It's all about the parsers. In some software with heavy parsers, that number will be much higher…anecdotally approaching 75 percent in some software we've seen.

- It's also all about the code—managed versus unmanaged, that is. Using managed code such as Java or C# will decrease the number of memory management flaws fuzzers are famous for finding.

- This figure is lower because Microsoft has many other avenues that contribute to security bug finding. In organizations without a formalized implementation of how security fits in the development process, the number would likely be higher, as these bugs would not be caught upstream of when the fuzzer is run.

Fuzzing Tools versus...

If you are running fuzzers, do you really need to acquire static code or runtime analysis tools? To our knowledge, no studies have been done to determine what number and types of bugs will be found when doing fuzzing versus code analysis tools. It's not an easy question to answer, as code bases will differ, as will the findings of different code analysis and fuzzing tools. Our recommendation is to use both, particularly if *any* the following are true.

> **The software has a large and complex code base.**   Especially if the code base has a large amount of legacy code that was written prior to security being a high priority in your organization.

> **The software was written in unmanaged code.**   Unmanaged code increases the risk of unintentional flaws being introduced due to memory management problems.

> **The software parses large amounts of user input.**   Obviously, the more data that's parsed, the higher the opportunity for mistakes.

> **The software has complex data structures.**   Complexity is the mating call of the promiscuous bug.

All code has bugs. Some bugs are security flaws. Software vendors should be diligent in protecting their users from unnecessary and avoidable vulnerabilities that lead to exploits. That said, do what's right for your customers.

Setting the Plan for Implementing Fuzzers into a Software Development Lifecycle

When embarking on the journey that is fuzzing, it's important as a software vendor to properly plan. There is a high likelihood that at some point someone externally will be running a fuzzer over your application, so it is imperative that you understand how your fuzzing effort will fit into your product's development lifecycle or risk public humiliation. Leaving it to be done ad-hoc means that there will likely be both duplicated efforts and uncovered testing—the latter of which will eventually bite you in the ass.

Setting Goals

Setting the goals for your fuzzing effort requires answering the questions "who," "what," "when," "how," and "why?" Why is covered earlier in this chapter and throughout the book, and the others are discussed here.

Fuzz Who?

Answering these questions will help the process of running fuzzers go more smoothly.

- Who owns defining the goals?
- Who owns setting the criteria and making the decision on which fuzzer to use? If the decision is to build it yourself, who owns building it?
- Who owns running the fuzzer?
- Who owns investigating, reproducing, and determining exploitability of the bugs found by the fuzzer?
- Who owns defining the criteria for which bugs found by the fuzzer will or will not be fixed?
- Who owns maintaining the fuzz testing infrastructure?

Another "who" type question is, "who in management is supporting this project?" We've seen or heard of a few cases where fuzzers were run late in the product cycle and found so many bugs that just doing the investigation of the issues would cause the product to slip. If you run into this problem, you'll need management support to help make a business decision of taking the risk of fixing these flaws late in the release cycle.

Fuzz What?

Defining the entry points into your application is one of the first steps in setting your team up for success. This should be part of any security test plan. *Hunting Security Bugs* by Gallagher, Landauer, and Jeffries has a great chapter on doing this. Once each entry point is defined and ranked based on risk, you'll be able to determine what you're going to fuzz. The more fuzzing done on the risky entry points, the better.

Here are some ideas of some typical entry points that have a moderate to high risk (depending on the programming language used):

- Network protocols (HTTP, SMTP, SIP, LDAP, etc.)

- RPCs

- Web services

- File formats (list them all, including those created outside your application that your software can import)

- ActiveX controls (OLE/COM Object Viewer) (www.microsoft.com/downloads/details.aspx?FamilyID=5233b70d-d9b2-4cb5-aeb6-45664be858b6&DisplayLang=en can help in finding these)

- Pluggable Web protocols (search the registry for "URL Protocol" to find cases of these; an example is telnet)

- Command-line parameters

NOTE

Do not forget the case where a malicious server may be sending the victim client bad data. In many client-server applications, this is a very common scenario (Web browsers being a common malicious server attack vector).

We should at least touch on the areas fuzzers are not as effective in, or are unimportant to focus your efforts on. We don't mean "fuzzers aren't good at finding vulnerability type <X>," but the areas of a product not worth looking at. First, never waste your time doing security testing using the application's client user interface. It holds true for general security testing as much as for fuzzing. You want to make sure your fuzzing is done at the level below where any client validation occurs. For example, in file fuzzing, you'll want to manipulate the bytes in the file directly and not waste your time twiddling things in the UI. Another area that can be difficult is where hardware meets software; for example, if you want to run fuzz tests on a hardware-based phone, but the phone needs user interaction (like picking up the handset) to accept the call. It's certainly not impossible to do fuzz testing on this area, but it requires things like automated robot arms or test hooks to pull off.

One other consideration is how to handle third-party code your application uses. What if your client software parses images (say it ships a copy of GDI+ or libPNG)?

Do you do fuzzing on that code base if it's a place an attacker can send malicious images to? Personally, we always feel better if we do assessments on the third-party code we use, including fuzzing, but it is always a lower priority than the code we are directly responsible for.

Fuzz When?

Determining when to start fuzzing depends on a number of things. If the code is legacy code that has already shipped and you want to start fuzzing that, you should start as soon as you can so any bugs found can be fixed either in the next version or in a service release or patch. In newly written code, though, it's important to start as early as possible in the release, but not too early. If you start too early, you'll risk testing areas that are partially implemented and raise the ire of your development team by opening bugs on unfinished code. Later in this chapter when we discuss generation versus mutation fuzzing, it will become clearer why starting too early can be a chore. Start too late and you'll run into even more serious problems. Why? Consider the following:

■ The "bouncer bug." This bug basically causes the majority of the code paths to be blocked. Sometimes, it can be worked around by tweaking the fuzzer to tone down the frequency or types of tests, but you don't want to hit this at the end of the development cycle, especially if it ends up requiring any significant changes that have a chance of being deferred to a future release.

■ Based on our experience, bugs found via fuzzing tend to be found in bunches. That's not a hard thing to imagine since a given developer will tend to make the same mistakes over and over again until he realizes the problem he is making. You'll find the first wave of fuzzing will find the highest number of bugs. Then once those bugs are fixed, the next wave will yield fewer bugs, continuing down the line until very few bugs are found in a given piece of software until a new set of features are added again.

■ Anyone who has worked for a software vendor understands that as the release date gets closer, the number of bugs that are allowed to be fixed decreases significantly to reduce potential regressions from occurring.

Fuzzing complex software is like washing your hair if you have obsessive compulsive disorder. Rinse, lather, repeat—times 10. There will need to be several iterations of bugs fixes and subsequent fuzzer runs to shake out the bugs.

In our opinion, the best time to insert fuzzing into your development cycle is when the code is stable enough that the feature(s) have been implemented and all major code paths can be exercised. The key is to continue to run your fuzzers throughout the product cycle so that even when new changes go into effect, the fuzzer is able to capture them (assuming your tests are updated as appropriate).

You may be wondering about the difference in integrating fuzzers into rapid release product cycles versus long multiyear ones. Certainly, shorter product cycles are a little trickier because of timing, but in the end the answer is the same. Run fuzzers as soon as the code is stable enough not to just be noise to the development team.

Fuzz How?

How, as in how do you decide whether to build your own fuzzer, buy a commercial one, or use a free version? Or how long should you run the fuzzer before moving on to the next area? How about different ways of increasing the number of fuzzer tests run? All interesting questions that we'll tackle next.

Buy, Build or Borrow?

Here's the big question: What fuzzer are you going to use, or will you build your own? We're not going to recommend a particular fuzzer or a group of fuzzers because every software vendor is in a slightly different situation. What we will do is list a few questions to investigate that will help guide you down the path to making an informed choice.

- What resources are available to you? Budget and time being the two biggest criteria here.

- What are you trying to fuzz? Commercial fuzzers are constantly expanding what they are able to fuzz, but they may not support your scenario just yet. Along the same lines, if you're trying to fuzz a proprietary format or protocol and want substantial coverage with your fuzzing, you'll likely need to build your own.

- What is the risk involved with the attack surface of the area you want to fuzz? Why spend lots of money on a commercial fuzzer if the area has limited risk? If it's a truly high-risk area, it's more reasonable to consider a larger budget.

- What is the extensibility of the fuzzer? There's several things to consider when evaluating extensibility:

- Extensibility is important when your product creates custom extensions on standards. If the fuzzer does not support extending its tests, you'll be missing a potentially large chunk of coverage.

- Sometimes you'll run across input used in an application that should rarely be changed. Fuzzers should support a notion of "value locking" that tells the fuzzer to not (or very rarely) alter a particular input. For example, in a Web application, the session ID would be such a field. Session ID is something that should be fuzzed, but consistently fuzzing that input when you want to increase your coverage will cause the user to be logged off, which will cause future tests to be less valid.

- For network fuzzing, it needs the capability to handle progressive steps. The fuzzer should be able to handle two aspects of this. First, it should support the capability to get a test ready to be fuzzed. The simplest example is that of authentication. If the fuzzer is sending malicious requests to an area that requires authentication, but no authentication has occurred yet, it will simply fail. The second aspect is about increasing your coverage. Some applications will require that events happen in a certain order. Hitting these code paths in a fuzzer requires that fuzzer to follow steps A then B then C and onward in order to hit that code path. For example, let's say that we want to add a new member to a distribution list. That member has a very long name and we're trying to determine if a buffer overrun exists in the server-side process of adding that new member. The fuzzer would first need to authenticate, if necessary, create the new member (with the long name), and then add that member to the distribution list.

- What type of bugs are you trying to find? Different fuzzers monitor for different types of flaws. Most will catch things like access violations and memory consumption issues, but will your application require more?

- Do you have control over what is fuzzed and what tests are possible? This could possibly fall under the extensibility category, but we've separated it out. The key question to ask here is whether the fuzzer will allow you to control things like frequency of injecting fuzzed data, what types of fuzzed data to use, or even what types of fuzzed data not to use. Each piece of software has its own data validation rules, and you'll want to make sure you can control the fuzzer enough so it's not exercising the same failure path excessively.

- What support level do you need? With commercial fuzzers, you're likely to get a decent level of support, as they'll want to keep your business. If you're using a free fuzzer off the Internet, support will vary considerably depending on the author. Obviously, building an in-house fuzzer means you're on the hook.

There is not always an easy answer for choosing which fuzzer to use. For the teams we've worked with in the past, we've investigated buying, but decided to build our own while also using any free fuzzers that would work with our feature set. For our situation, this worked well.

How Long to Run the Fuzzer

A very valid question that always causes much discussion is, "How long should we run our fuzzers?" or "How many iterations of the fuzzer should we submit our product to?" Microsoft's Security Development Lifecycle documentation states that all file parsers and formats it releases must go through 100,000 iterations in order to ship—100,000 is not an arbitrary number. Whatever the number is, it needs to be something product teams can accomplish, but large enough that it would catch a significant number of flaws. What we believe is more important is that the iterations need to be *clean*. This means no bugs are found in the 100,000 iterations (aside from the few known unexploitable issues). To get to this point you've probably run through many sets of 100,000 iterations, as each time you run the fuzzer it finds different flaws that are then fixed. The next fuzzer run then gets down further code paths and finds issues in those areas. This process continues until the format can get through 100,000 clean iterations. If you're setting goals within your corporation, it's important to stress the notion of clean runs.

With all this said, the number of clean runs you should require for a particular area to be fuzzed is relative to the complexity of that area. It would be insane to require a fuzzer to be run 100,000 times on a Web page with one single string as input, but 100,000 is perfectly reasonable for a complex file format with complex data structures. We don't quibble over these types of numbers and have generally taken a different approach. Fuzz your software all day, all night, on as many machines as you can. Hey, it's free testing…why not?

Shaking the Bug Tree

As mentioned earlier, each time the development team fixes a set of bugs found by a fuzzer, they are opening up new code paths that may also contain bugs. It's important to note this, as running a fuzzer just once or twice may not uncover the full set of bugs it is capable of finding. Figure 7.2 shows a theoretical bug trend chart. On the Y-axis you have the number of bugs found. On the x-axis, you have the number of fuzzer passes where one pass is dependent on the previous pass's bugs being fixed. While the graph is theoretical, it is empirical based on our prior experience. The bug line appears to decrease close to exponentially and points out that each pass will typically yield less bugs, but over the long haul may come across a small number of issues as testing continues.

The key point not being that you'll find 25 bugs on your first pass (or even more or less than that), but that as developers fix bugs, the fuzzer is able to flex more code.

NOTE

There is an implicit assumption in the graph in Figure 7.2: the fuzzer is being run when the code is relatively stable. If the code were changing rapidly with new features being added after past fuzzer passes, it would not be abnormal to see spikes in future passes. The other aspect that can skew this data is if you are updating your fuzzer with new tests or new methods for monitoring for vulnerabilities.

Figure 7.2 Theoretical Bug Trend Chart

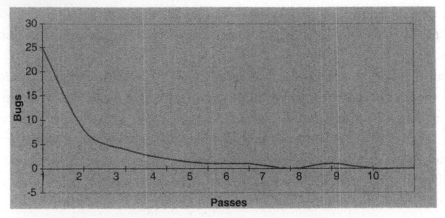

Increasing Fuzzer Coverage

Let's say you want to increase the number of fuzzer runs on your software. What are your options?

24/7

The easiest and simplest way to get more fuzzer coverage is to run your fuzzers 24 hours a day, 7 days a week.

Distributed Fuzzing

You have co-workers who go home at some point in the night. Why not, when they head home, have them kick off a script that uses their machine to power your fuzzer.

Integrating Fuzzers into Stress Runs

Many software vendors that ship servers (or services) have a notion of stress testing. This involves a production-like environment set up to see how long the server can withstand usage beyond the normal capacity, the goal being to use this information to deduce robustness and availability of your servers. You could say that fuzz testing is a way to put your servers under intense stress!

Getting your fuzzers hooked up in this scenario may require the same steps as doing distributed fuzzing. Running continuous fuzz testing in your stress environment may have undesired hidden costs depending on the fuzzer being used. Those hidden costs are covered later in this chapter.

Building and Executing on the Plan

Once you've answered the basic questions listed previously you should be in a good position to start the process of integrating fuzzing into your software development lifecycle. We've broken the process into three sections.

- Building the plan
- Running the fuzzer through the release
- Postmortem analysis

Building the Plan

Ideally, this documentation should happen early in a product cycle, toward the middle to end of the design phase. You could start earlier for legacy features, but for newer features you'll want to have a good idea of the technology bets your product will be taking. The fuzzing plan may bleed into the coding stage of the product cycle as plans are firmed up. Keep in mind that as the product evolves, the fuzzing plan should too. Changes in direction by the product team may significantly impact your planning.

The following sidebar is a sample fuzzing plan for a small feature. You could use it to write the fuzzing plan for a particular feature, but more likely, you would write it for an entire piece of software. We chose to write this for a feature for the sake of brevity.

Tools & Traps...

Sample Fuzzing Plan

Fuzzing Plan for Acme Software: ISAPI filter
Jon Smith
1/29/2008

Summary

Acme Software is producing an ISAPI filter used for authenticating users to be released in December 2008. It is written in unmanaged code and will have entry points that are anonymously accessible by anyone on the Internet. As such, it's important that a solid plan be in place for solid security analysis, one piece of which is fuzzing.

Goals

Reduce costs of security testing by feature team by 50%
Find vulnerabilities in our software prior to release
Run at least 50,000 fuzzer tests on filter

Plan

Areas Covered
Login entry point
Logout entry point
Session Identifier

Areas Not Covered
Cryptanalysis of session identifier creation
Logic and design flaws in how session identifier is issued and maintained
Login transport security

These areas will be covered through manual security testing and code reviews. See test case management tests 1192 through 1213 for a complete set of manual security test cases for this feature.

Tools Used

Internal Acme Software fuzzer will be used in this testing. It is currently under development and should be finished by 2/15/2008.

Timeline

The development team believes the feature should be stable enough and feature complete by April 2008. At that point, we will begin fuzzing and run the fuzzer throughout the release. To help increase coverage we will distribute the load of the fuzzer across our engineering team, having each member run the fuzzer at night when he goes home. This way, we should easily meet the 50,000 goal.

Ownership

Project Owner: Jon Smith
Stakeholders: Software Development and Test teams
Sponsor: Suraj Poozhiyil

Results

TBD once testing is finished.

Once you've completed the plan, you'll need to sell it to your management team, as there is a cost to doing this work. Focus on what your audience cares about. Some specific examples may include:

- The amount of coverage the fuzzer will give (managers tend to be impressed when you tell them the fuzzer will run through XXXXXXX number of automated tests on your software with little human interaction)

- The amount of time it will save the development and test team

- The cost of not doing this work (for example, if someone external uses this method to find vulnerabilities)

- Any information you can find on bugs being found externally by fuzzers in your or your competitor's products

- Data on how many and what percentage of the previous release's vulnerabilities could have been found by fuzzers

If you have the data and can market the solution, this should not be a terribly hard sell. The number of flaws found by fuzzers and the reduction in cost in security testing should be enough to get your plan approved.

NOTE

If you run into roadblocks the first time you present to your management team, you may need to do further analysis. Try to get a trial version of a commercial fuzzer, or use a free fuzzer from the Internet to see what bugs the fuzzer is able to uncover in a particular area. Having data about your specific product will hit closer to home with managers. With heavy pushback, it never hurts to write an exploit to show the dangers of the flaws being found.

Running the Fuzzer through the Release

After your plan is approved, you'll need to execute it. The basic execution of the fuzzer is dependent on that particular fuzzer, and we won't dive into that here, except to say, a) keep the fuzzer running as often as possible, and b) keep the builds you're running it on updated. As discussed earlier in the chapter, this stage should start as soon as the product is stable enough to handle malicious input being thrown at it.

NOTE

In past lives, our teams have had separate banks of machines to do our fuzzing. We had a fairly complex setup with multiple servers and multiple clients. Part of our fuzzing plan was the requisition of these machines. On the flipside, doing file format fuzzing can easily be done on a single box.

Prior to the initial runs of the fuzzer, we recommend communicating the fuzzing plan for the engineering team responsible for the software. Let them know that it's undetermined how many issues the fuzzer will find, but to be on the lookout for any bugs opened. You may also want to get buyoff from your management team to make sure a certain priority is placed on getting these bugs fixed quickly so they do not block further fuzz testing.

Beyond maintaining the infrastructure for running the fuzzing test infrastructure, the big cost in this stage is investigating any issues the fuzzer finds. Put a priority on making sure these are thoroughly investigated with the steps to reproduce them narrowed down as much as possible. Also, make sure you give the development team all the information they need to easily reproduce the flaws. When the question of exploitability comes up, you may also be brought in to provide input.

In any organization, it is important to make the progress on the security front visible to the individuals on the team. We suggest documenting status on your fuzzing efforts into any security status mail sent throughout the release or any security status presentations. This will give visibility to the work being done, and give the engineers a better understanding of what types of issues the fuzzers are and are not finding.

Postmortem Analysis

The postmortem analysis of your fuzzer(s) can occur at any time during the product cycle, but is typically well situated toward the end. Once you've completed a full release of fuzzing, you'll have a good idea of what bugs it did well at finding and those it did not. Start by bucketing all the security flaws not found by the fuzzer by vulnerability type and then brainstorming ways you can build cases to test for and discover these flaws. As mentioned previously, some bugs types are not easily found by fuzzing and require threat modeling, manual security testing, source code review, or other tools to discover them.

NOTE

> Personally, we find it useful to monitor the bug tracking system daily to determine what security bugs have been found. For each of them we ask the question, "why didn't the fuzzer find the flaw and could it be updated to do so?

Understanding How to Increase Effectiveness of Fuzzers, and Avoiding Any Big Gotchas

Over time, as you continue running fuzzers you'll notice a couple of things. First, some costs with running them aren't necessarily clear up front. Second, fuzzers can hit points where they find very few bugs. In this next section, we discuss what costs you'll encounter as you run fuzzers throughout a release, and some different steps you can take to increase their bug-finding capability when the first wave of bugs stops pouring in.

Hidden Costs

Although running fuzzers may seem like the holy grail of software security testing, there are certainly costs associated with it that may make you rue the day you first ran it. All of these hidden costs are issues we've hit personally, so we've written them in the form of a dialogue.

Reproducing Bugs

Not Us: Hey, our fuzzer caused the server to crash.

Us: Cool, how?

Not Us: Hmmm…I don't know.

Reproducing bugs can be a major pain (especially with network fuzzing). Keeping a debugger attached to the processes you're monitoring can help, but it's not a failsafe. Sending the developer a call stack may not be enough, as they may want the specific steps required to reproduce the flaw. We've certainly come across cases where finding the bugs was not as simple as replaying a single packet. The application was in a state where multiple packets caused the server to get into an invalid state.

The other aspect of this is you need to keep good logs of what was tested (and what was fuzzed). Without good logging, you're really up the creek without a paddle for more complicated bugs. However, even with this information, nailing down a bug can sometimes be an all-day event.

Investigating Bugs

Not Us: Hey, our fuzzer found 200 crashes last night.

Us: Holy crap…

Not Us: What should I do?

Us: Are they different call stacks?

Not Us: Yeah.

Us: Have you looked into the exploitability of them?

Not US: I looked at a few…half were exploitable, the other ones I'm not sure yet.

Us: …

Us: …

Us: We should talk to the development manager to let him know what we've found. Open a bug in the meantime to track this.

Not Us: Ok.

[later that day]

Development Manager: We don't have time to fix all of these, let alone investigate whether they are exploitable.

Us: As painful as it may be, we have to investigate them. We've already found a good portion of the ones we've investigated to be exploitable. The risk involved with not fixing these far outweighs the potential cost of investigation.

[conversation continues … usually a long time ☺]

This conversation is really pointing at three things:

- Sometimes you'll be overwhelmed by the number of flaws found. This particularly happens in complex legacy code bases. In our experience, complex file formats tend to be major offenders.

- When you suddenly drop a boatload of bugs on a developer, he will not be happy. Just going through the call stacks of all 200 bugs would be very time consuming. Sometimes, there are ways a development team can systematically eliminate these types of issues, sometimes not.

- Determining exploitability on 200 bugs is extremely costly. If you are the individual responsible for running the fuzzer, you may be involved by proxy in the investigation of exploitability.

Make sure to allocate time in your schedule for investigation of the bugs found via your fuzzers.

> **NOTE**
>
> The best policy for exploitability is if you don't know whether it's exploitable, just fix it!

Bad Assumptions

Tester: I think it's so cool that your fuzzer does all my security testing for me.

Us: Uh…no it doesn't.

Tester: Sure, I took a look at all the bugs it found and I would just be duplicating the effort of the fuzzer with my testing.

Us: Do you understand exactly what code paths in your feature the fuzzer executes? Do you know explicitly what tests it tries on those code paths? Do you know what types of bugs it monitors for?

Tester: Not exactly.

When software engineers see bugs being opened in a given area, they assume it's being covered—a dangerous assumption when it comes to fuzz testing. Do *not* rely on fuzzers to do all your security testing. Stress to your test team what types of vulnerabilities the fuzzer can find and what limitations it has. Have them focus the majority of their time on the areas the fuzzer is not effective at hitting.

Reports

Manager: How do we know whether we've hit our fuzzing goals? Is there a status server somewhere?

Us: We could build one...

Obviously, if your organization is setting goals around fuzzing some level of reporting of status against those goals is important. Keeping it simple is fine. In the past, the format in Figure 7.3 has worked well for us.

Figure 7.3 Status Report

Area	Iterations	Goal	Bugs Found
Web Services			
AddUser	4500	10000	3 <links>
DeleteUser	2000	10000	0
...			
ActiveX Controls			
FOO.ProgID	23500	50000	4 <links>
BAR.ProgID	43800	50000	2 <links>
...			

Purchasing a commercial fuzzer may come with a much more advanced set of reports.

Software Gotchas

Not Us: I don't think our fuzzer is working.

Us: What do you mean?

Not Us: It didn't find any bugs and it ran all last week!

Us: Maybe the code is solid…or maybe we're not really testing anything. Let's look at the logs.

[time passes]

Not Us: Looks like we're getting logged out every time we fuzz a packet to the server.

Us: Yeah, the server must be doing some heavy validation, or we're invalidating a checksum with the data we're sending.

It can be very frustrating to realize that partway through your fuzzing effort you missed something key in how the software handles malicious packets. In the preceding case in a server product, the server was doing several things: limiting the size of the packets, limiting the number of headers, limiting the characters used in the packet, and more. Our fuzzer had no prior knowledge of this so we ended up only testing the initial validation happening on the packet without going deep down the code paths we wanted to. The server simply logged us out.

Another area where you'll run into problems if you're doing mutation fuzzing with proxies (discussed later in this chapter) is with checksums. If there is a checksum on the data you are altering, you'll need to recreate a new checksum on the altered data.

Each piece of software will be different as far as gotchas are concerned. Enter fuzzing with your eyes open to these potential problematic areas.

Finding More Vulnerabilities

As you go through a release or two using fuzzing tools, you'll start to ask some deeper questions as fewer bugs are found via your fuzzer. First, are you getting the depth of coverage you want, or are you hitting the same code paths over and over again? Second, even if you hit an application bug, would your fuzzer know what it meant, or would it happily ignore it because the software didn't crash? Third, is it worthwhile to run more than one fuzzer?

Increasing Coverage

One of the goals of any good fuzzing strategy is to look for ways to increase the coverage of your fuzzer. We're going to reiterate briefly the different types of fuzzing discussed earlier in the book, touch on the pros and cons of each, and discuss what type of coverage on your applications each is better for. The four techniques are generation, mutation, smart, and dumb.

Generation

Generation fuzzing is when your fuzzer is solely responsible for generating the input sent to the application. It can be very powerful, but requires in-depth knowledge of the file format or network protocol.

Pros

- Gives the most control to the implementer.
- You know exactly what you're testing.

Cons

- Requires the most in-depth knowledge up front.
- Requires the largest amount of development time.
- Changes in the file format or network protocol may cause breaking changes or may lead to missed testing.

Mutation

Mutation fuzzing is taking already existing valid data and altering aspects of it to be invalid and/or malicious. It is also very powerful and generally requires less upfront knowledge of the file format or network protocol.

Pros

- Gives a large amount of control to the implementer.
- Easy to get up and running quickly.
- Maintenance is relatively easy.
- Gives the highest amount of code coverage with the least amount of work.

Cons

- Getting the right set of templates to use for file formats and network packets can be problematic. This can lead to missed and duplicated testing, as the individual the running fuzzer may not be as aware of the file format or protocol he is testing.
- Certain test cases tend to be ignored; for example, send malicious packet X 1000 times.
- Reproducing bugs can be more painful.

Smart

Smart fuzzing, also known as intelligent fuzzing, is when the fuzzer has built-in knowledge of the file format or network protocol. It allows for deeper code path penetration.

Pros

- Tends to go deeper into code paths.
- Requires more in-depth knowledge of the file format or network protocol.

Cons

- Time required to invest in file format or network protocol knowledge.
- Smart fuzzers can be too smart for their own good. There's a balance in all fuzzers of how much of a packet to keep valid and how much to change. Often, smart fuzzers lean toward keeping the file format or packet too clean.

Dumb

Dumb fuzzing has no knowledge of the file format or network protocol and simply sends random data. Surprisingly, this technique finds bugs.

Pros

- Implementation cost is low.

Cons

- Tends to find low-hanging fruit quickly and then fails to find further deeper bugs.

Where to Focus Time

For maximum coverage in your application, a mixture of these techniques is needed. If you're looking to build your own fuzzer for your organization where one does not already exist, the quickest way is to build a dumb-mutation fuzzer. It's not guaranteed to find all the bugs, but at the very least, you're on the path to building a better fuzzer, which increases the coverage substantially.

> **NOTE**
>
> We've personally worked on a lot of client-server software. We've built man-in-the-middle capture and edit proxies for any network protocols we use. This is to help the test team become more familiar with the protocols their features use and to do their security testing below any client-side validation. The proxies sit on the client machines and capture the packets prior to being sent to the server (or on the other side, they capture the server packets before the client receives them).
>
> Network proxies are great tools for building smart (or dumb) network mutation fuzzers. When the proxies receive the traffic, it is completely valid and can be handed off to the fuzzer to create a malicious packet and reinjected before it goes back to the server or client.
>
> The best part about this is that you can reuse any test automation you've already written to help drive traffic. Keep in mind, though, that areas that are not automated will get no coverage and your test automation may or may not be robust enough to handle some of the errors caused by fuzzing.
>
> Using network proxies to do fuzzing does not work well for a few cases like:
>
> - DoS attacks that send the same packet multiple times
> - Replaying or dropping packets
> - Out of sequence packets

Code Coverage

A solid way to measure your fuzzer's effectiveness or lack thereof is by using code coverage. Code coverage is a mechanism used to give you a measurement of the level of code paths you are executing during testing. Code coverage can be used for automated testing or manual testing. In this case, we'll use it for fuzzing.

There are numerous code coverage tools available on the Web. We will not be doing an analysis of the best code coverage tools to use, as that is dependent on your project and not in the scope of this book.

Once we've run our code coverage tools we'll get an idea of what code paths we exercised and those we didn't. For those we didn't, we can analyze why we didn't hit them by looking directly at the code and determining if it is possible and worth the time for us to update the fuzzer to go down these paths. In the following sample code, we'll need to change our fuzzer slightly to handle a custom extension that brings us down a conditional path.

```
public string getStatus(string userName, request headers)
{
  if(headers.getValue("x-corp-foo") == "bar")
  {
    //some code path we weren't hitting with the fuzzer as
    //the fuzzer has no knowledge of this custom header value
    //or the fact that it must be set to "bar" to hit it.
  }
  //more getStatus code...
}
```

In the past, we've heard individuals state that they want to get to 100% code coverage with their fuzzer. Depending on your application, the actual percentage you get up to may not be interesting at all.

For example, in an application that's sole responsibility is to be a parser of network traffic, it makes sense to try to hit all code paths for the part of the code that receives packets coming from untrusted sources. However, in an application like Adobe Acrobat, the number is uninteresting on the code path that handles Find and Replace in a PDF or the code path that handles setup, as there is likely no user input that goes into these code paths that is controlled by an attacker.

Increasing code coverage is a good thing, but set realistic goals for your application.

Running More than One Fuzzer

No metric exists today to measure the effectiveness of one fuzzer over another. Even if one did exist, we don't think we'd believe it. Most fuzzers are similar in nature, in the same way Microsoft's Hotmail and Google's GMail are both Web-based e-mail software, but under the hood the code is completely different. We mention this because different authors of fuzzers take different approaches. Some favor brute force methods over randomness. Some rely more heavily on keeping packets and file formats valid versus taking a bazooka approach. Some were built to find memory-based flaws, while others may have the capability to detect protocol-specific issues. As such, it's not a bad idea to consider running more than one fuzzer over your areas of interest.

Generally, running another fuzzer doesn't induce that much more pain (especially if you've fixed all the low-hanging fruit already). It will also give you confidence in your application, as folks outside your corporation will run these externally available fuzzers over your software. If your original fuzzer was well written, in all likelihood very little will be found, but you'll sleep better at night knowing you've done that extra work.

Monitoring

Two major pieces of building a fuzzer (or questions to ask when buying or using a free one) are deciding what malicious input to send and how to determine whether that malicious input caused a software flaw. We believe that a big part of the future of fuzzing is going to be building better monitoring systems, especially on software that is more than mildly complex.

For the first fuzzer we helped design, one of the first things we did was list the entry points we wanted to focus on, and then listed the types of vulnerabilities it may be susceptible to. For any C/C++ application, you have your basics: buffer overruns, integer overflows, format strings, etc. For any Web applications: cross-site scripting, SQL injection, etc. After going through all the common attacks for the areas, we brainstormed more application- or implementation-specific flaws. For example, elevation of privilege attacks on our Web application or accessing arbitrary files in a safe for scripting ActiveX control. Once we had this list, we went through and listed all the mechanisms we had for detecting these bugs. In some cases, something already existed; in others, we had to write our own code; and in a couple cases, the ability and cost of detecting the flaw was either fraught with error or much too costly.

To illustrate our point, let's look at one example of how one could detect a certain type of bug. With a little ingenuity, most vulnerability types can be detected. Earlier, we mentioned elevation of privilege attacks in a Web application. For the sake of argument, let's say that this is a banking application, and the key thing being protected is that user A should never be able to see user B's data. Effectively, we are testing the Web application's handling of authorization. Vulnerabilities that lead to this type of disclosure are usually parameter tampering attacks (or session ID tampering, but we'll exclude that for now). For example, in the URL http://bank.example.com/transaction.jsp?transactionid=324569, we may try changing the transactionid value to something above or below the integer currently used to see if we are able to gain access to someone else's account data. Depending on the application, we have several potential options to determine if our fuzzer is able to find such vulnerabilities by monitoring HTTP responses:

- Once logged in, most banking applications will include the account number or username of the logged-in user. If the response contains something out of the norm, we may have hit a vulnerability.

- If the previous example will not work with your application, you can try seeding the data store. What we mean by this is that you can find a piece (or pieces) of input you know is rendered back in most if not all pages. Knowing that, you can add a marker to the data owned by users other than user A that the malicious user should never see (in this case, you'd need to seed for much more then one user); for example, adding "!!!" preceding the particular data you're interested in. Now you'll need to build a simple monitor piece for the fuzzer, which analyzes the response looking for "!!!". If you see it, you know that a vulnerability has been found.

Once you have a good feel for the types of vulnerabilities your application exhibits, spend the time to determine whether your fuzzer(s) is able to detect such flaws. If not, hopefully there is a mechanism to extend its functionality to monitor for new types of vulnerabilities.

Summary

As you've read through this book, you've no doubt seen the powerful nature of fuzzers. Many software vendors are beginning to realize that fuzzing can be a very fruitful method of detecting vulnerabilities prior to releasing products to customers. For those vendors for whom this is not obvious, it should become so very quickly as external security researchers, corporations evaluating software packages, and those with malicious intent begin using fuzzers on their software.

While fuzzers are a very effective mechanism for finding bugs quickly and reducing testing costs, it's also important to note that running fuzzers in the absence of a broader security policy will not give you a complete security story. Fuzzers are very good at finding certain types of vulnerabilities, while others are better left to tasks such as threat modeling or penetration testing.

As you begin to integrate fuzzing into your software development lifecycle, keep in mind that any plans should be organic. The best fuzzers are those that are updated to better facilitate the testing of your applications. As new attacks are found by security researchers and new techniques are found for detecting bugs, update your fuzzer periodically to keep the testing fresh.

Solutions Fast Track

Why Is Fuzzing Important to Include in a Software Development Cycle?

- ☑ Fuzzers are a very effective method for finding bugs in software that relies heavily on parsers. The more complex the parsers, the more likely fuzzers will find many issues.

- ☑ Doing manual security testing is extremely time consuming. Fuzzers can help in offloading much of that process and provide better coverage for certain types of testing.

- ☑ If your software is widely deployed, individuals external to your organization will be running fuzzers against your software. It's that simple. Do you want to be publicly embarrassed, or would you rather find these flaws in house before you have to deal with hot fix or patching nightmares?

- ☑ It is understood that the cost of fixing a bug once a product has already been released increases substantially. The last thing you want to deal with is 50 vulnerabilities in your software reported externally because someone ran a fuzzer over your file format. You'll have customers demanding patches *right now*, and some making the decision to switch from your software to a competitor's.

Setting Expectations for Fuzzers in a Software Development Lifecycle

☑ Integrating fuzzing into your software development lifecycle because it's a popular technique is not a good idea. It needs to be carefully considered based on the technologies and languages you are using, and be part of a formalized security process. Simply running fuzzers on your software will not produce secure code. With that said, fuzzers can be a major piece of moving in the right direction toward more secure code if the right set of additional security policies and practices is in place.

☑ Fuzzing tools are not meant to find all known vulnerabilities. Depending on the complexity of your application, you may very well need to extend them to meet your needs. Even after that is finished, tasks such as Threat Modeling, security code reviews, and penetration testing will help round out your security plan.

☑ Substituting fuzzers for source code analysis tools is not a good idea. The opposite is true as well. Fuzzers and source code analysis tools will find some of the same bugs, but will also uncover unique flaws.

Setting the Plan for Implementing Fuzzers into a Software Development Lifecycle

☑ Setting the goals of what you'd like to accomplish with the use of fuzzers is a good first step toward building a solid fuzzing plan. Without a solid list of goals or expectations, it will be difficult to measure whether the process was a success.

☑ When creating the plan for running a fuzzer(s), you'll need to answer the question of ownership on many levels: who will be responsible for choosing the fuzzer, maintaining the infrastructure to run it, opening and investigating flaws found by it, and more.

☑ Your fuzzer plan should also include answers to what specifically you will be fuzzing and the risks associated with those areas. This will help in your prioritization exercises later.

☑ You'll need to consider when to perform fuzz testing. Starting too late can lead to missed bugs, but starting too early can lead to an unhappy development team, as code may not be ready for the harshness of that type of testing.

☑ You'll need to carefully consider what fuzzer(s) meets your requirements for the areas you are interested in testing. There are numerous commercial fuzzers available at a cost. Free ones can also be found quite easily on the Internet. Alternatively, you may be interested in building your own if one does not exist for what you are attempting to test. Depending on the file format or network protocol you are testing, you may take a mixed approach.

Understanding How to Increase Effectiveness of Fuzzers, and Avoiding any Big Gotchas

☑ There are several hidden costs to running fuzzers as a software vendor that may not be blatantly obvious. Reproducing bugs can be problematic if your fuzzer doesn't contain solid logging or the issue requires several prior failures to get into that state. If the fuzzer comes across a number of bugs, investigating them and determining exploitability can be a huge cost. This is more common to see on legacy code that has not been through a more formalized security process. Be careful if your development or test team starts looking at the fuzzer as the ultimate authority on the security of the product. Watch out for comments where they feel it's not important to do security code reviews or security testing because "the fuzzer has it covered." Stress to them what the fuzzer does find and what it does not. All software has its own set of validation rules and logic for when it receives potentially malicious data. You may have to alter your fuzzer so that at least part of the time it plays within those rules so the fuzzer can reach deeper code paths.

☑ There are different techniques for increasing the number of flaws found by fuzzing. One of the important areas to focus is on making sure you are able to detect when certain types of bugs are hit. Crashes are easy to monitor for, but other types of bugs (and implementation specific bugs) may require you to extend your fuzzer. There are generally four techniques used for fuzzing: generation, mutation, smart, and dumb. Understanding where these techniques work well and don't work well is important. If your fuzzer is relying heavily on a particular technique and is not finding many bugs, we suggest trying a different technique.

☑ Using code coverage can be a useful way to determine what code paths your fuzzer is not hitting. Understanding this you can alter the fuzzer in different ways that help guide it down those other paths. Don't worry about hitting 100% code coverage in most software, as what you're really worried about is that you get coverage on the pieces of code where malicious input can enter.

Frequently Asked Questions

Q: We ran the fuzzer right before we released and it found lots of bugs…we fixed those but we don't have time to run any more tests…is that ok?

A: Fuzzing tends to find bugs in bunches. The short answer is that if you found many bugs in the first run, you're likely to find many bugs (less, but still quite a few) in subsequent runs once those original flaws are fixed.

Q: Why should I spend money on a commercial fuzzer when there's many free ones?

A: Some of the free versions are very intuitive and easy to use—some, not so much. The support level of free fuzzers can also vary depending on the responsiveness of the developer. They may not care much if you're shipping your product in three weeks and you need them to fix a bug in their fuzzer. The quality of the free fuzzers also varies significantly. Personally, we recommend evaluating the free versions available, and if it works for your situation, great. If not, consider buying a commercial version or building your own if you have the technical expertise to do so.

Q: How much time and money should I budget?

A: Time will depend on several factors. Will you buy, build, or use a free fuzzer? How large is the code base? How much of it is legacy code? Is the software written in managed or unmanaged code? What is the attack surface of the product? How many areas are you planning to fuzz? There are the hidden costs of bug investigation as well. Money basically boils down to whether you'll buy a commercial version of a fuzzer.

Q: My fuzzer hasn't found anything in the last several months of running it…what gives?

A: It could mean several things. It could be that your fuzzer isn't executing any new code paths. It could be that your fuzzer is failing on some initial validation the application does. Or it could be that the code has solid protection against the attacks your fuzzer is testing. We suggest trying two things: 1) Run code coverage tools to determine which code paths you are failing to hit and tweak your fuzzer as necessary, and 2) If another fuzzer is applicable that supports your file format or network protocol and is free, give it a shot.

Q: Is fuzzer X better than fuzzer Y?

A: We have no idea. Your best bet is trying each on your application to see if it meets the requirements and goals you've set in your initial fuzzer planning.

Q: I work in a very small development shop. Should I be using fuzzing?

A: They key is to weigh how much security analysis your product will need. If it's heavy into parsing and has interesting attack vectors, it is definitely worth performing fuzz testing. If the software is a simple stand-alone client application (say, a children's game) without any attack vectors, you know the answer to the question. The answer is not always black and white, though. Our advice would be to lean toward the cautious side for a couple of reasons: a) the cost of issuing patches on externally found vulnerabilities can be very costly for you and your customers, and b) fuzzers are getting to the point where all it takes is five minutes to get one up and running on well-known protocols or file formats. It would take you a short time to get set up, but the flipside is that the bar is very low for an attacker to get started too.

Fuzzing and the Corporate Environment

Chapter 8

Standardization and Certification

Solutions in this chapter:

- Fuzzing and the Corporate Environment
- Software Security Testing, the Challenges
- Testing for Security
- Fuzzing as a Viable Option

Fuzzing and the Corporate Environment

Fuzzing is a black-box testing technique, today, mostly for software. Therefore, it makes perfect sense for this technology to be used by software developers and software vendors for their QA and testing. In the corporate environment, it would make perfect sense for fuzzing to be used specifically for that—testing and proofing new applications.

There are other uses for fuzzing in the corporate environment, some of which have far-reaching implications. Most corporations, or organizations for that matter, have an IT infrastructure such as a network, a Web page, an e-mail system, etc. This infrastructure is sometimes built without security considerations, based on basic needs put together or against budgetary concerns and functional needs. When the organization is about to buy a new product, it will proceed through different bureaucratic channels of varying complexity, and eventually decide on a product.

The technological evaluation part of that process varies, and can be as significant as it can be discarded. In some cases, the product is put through its paces in a demo or a pilot and tested to see if it is stable and provides all the requirements.

How the product is tested for security, stability, and usage is what we discuss in this chapter, and what implications this testing may have on the software industry.

When it comes to security, the testing often ends with a list of security features on a marketing checklist and the check that they are there. How do you test a product to see if it is secure itself? What implications can such testing have on the software world?

Up to now we discussed the concept of *fuzz before release*; now we will discuss the concept of *fuzz before purchase*. We will explore the caveats to the second approach, and how it can help your business save costs and pass audits. That and more is discussed in this chapter.

The concept of standardizing how fuzz testing is done is beyond the scope of this chapter, and is far away in terms of likelihood.

Software Security Testing, the Challenges

Software security testing has always been problematic, at least for the end clients who do not always have the luxury of looking at the source code.

Without the source code, security testing requires highly skilled professionals in the difficult and expensive niche of reverse engineering. It requires specially built labs to put products through stress testing, simulated regular usage, attacks, etc. All in all, the results of such tests, depending on the resources invested, would be anywhere from worthless to very good.

This is an expensive and time-consuming process, and when done, can never be announced as complete. Much like any testing, it can speak to the quality of the software and its stability; it cannot guarantee that there will be no vulnerabilities in it.

The prohibitive cost combined with imperfect results and potential liability for the tester, both from the client (who may sue if vulnerabilities are later disclosed) and from the vendor (who may sue for intellectual property violations or for any other number of reasons) caused the field of security testing for products to die out.

Those who do provide such services do it direct-to-client as a service and in most cases will not publicize their results. Others include very large organizations that have specialized testing teams.

One type of security testing for products that is widely accepted, and very controversial, is antivirus testing, which we discuss at the end of this chapter as an example of further challenges and some solutions.

Testing for Security

Before we continue and discuss how fuzzing presents itself as a viable option for software testing for end clients, we'll examine how such testing is done today.

In this case, we are not speaking of reverse engineering and costly software testing, but rather of simple tasks that can be performed before a product is chosen.

There are many methods for such testing, such as a pilot run and user simulation, but some of the ones specific to security repeat in most organizations that perform such testing. We will cover a few.

Historical Studies

Of course, learning from history is always useful. Searching through bugtraq and other historical vulnerability information sources such as SecuriTeam for old vulnerabilities in the product we test can at times prove very useful.

Problems with such information include:

- Out-of-date data
- Metrics and terminology differ considerably between reports
- Data is not always verified or verifiable

- Reports are on different product versions or code bases

- Not all products meet with the same scrutiny from the researcher community

Therefore, although vulnerability history does give us a glimpse into the product's security and the company's coding standards, it is far from reliable, if it exists. And then, it is often too scattered both in content and context to be useful for such a study.

Further, our premise when doing such research should be: information may not exist, and if it does, it will not be conclusive.

Edge cases exist with products that have been heavily scrutinized (many different reports over time) or studied (researched specifically), and are most useful.

Although the information gathered and conclusions reached are far from perfect, they are important. They can indicate issues not necessarily relating to how securely the code was built, but rather how scrutinized it is (how popular) and how much attention it gets from the research community. Are there new vulnerabilities disclosed often? Are these then critical?

With all the caveats, this method is the best one that exists today other than performing your own exhaustive and resource consuming testing.

Stress Testing

Stress testing is an accepted and long practiced method of testing new products, especially when it comes to network services.

The service would be bombarded by a large number of requests, up to a point where it could no longer handle them. This helps with tweaking configuration so more queries can be handled, and to make sure the server can handle what it will face.

Stress testing can be considered, to a very limited degree, fuzzing. It sends large amounts of requests, which can also result in issues such as hangs and crashes.

Vulnerability Scanning

Vulnerability scanning (also known as vulnerability assessment) is used for network security, searching for insecure computers and missing patches on them.

Vulnerability scanning is not specific to product testing and, to be honest, is not very useful for it. It was never meant to be used as such as it can only provide very limited results.

It isn't meant to find new vulnerabilities or test for robustness.

There are two goals one can hope to reach:

- Fuzzing for the very poor: see if an old vulnerability triggers a new one.

- If the product comes as an appliance, see that the operating system and applications on it are properly secure and hardened.

To a very limited degree, scanning for open ports can also be useful for seeing if the operating system and other applications have been secure.

Fuzzing as a Viable Option

With all the difficulties and price tag of software security testing done without source code, as important as it may be, it has been largely neglected. Fuzzing technology comes as a viable alternative to some of these, with a lower cost and faster results.

Fuzzing first entered the scene as a technique used by hackers, or as homegrown tools used mostly by large vendors for specialized security testing. With the fuzzing industry maturing and the introduction of easy-to-use products, fuzzing presents itself as a viable option for organizations that do not have the source code and are looking to test before they buy.

Here are the main reasons fuzzing may just make such testing an option:

- Fuzzing is black-box testing, which means *no source code is required*.

- Automated fuzzing is doable to a large extent.

- Fuzzing in its simplest form indicates *critical bugs, such as crashes and hangs*, which can of course also mean *vulnerabilities*.

- Fuzzing can indicate the *stability and robustness of a product*: how often does it crash? What does it take to crash it?

- Most importantly, fuzzing is low-cost and easily repeatable.

For these reasons, fuzzing presents itself as a viable option for testing new products before they are purchased, and knowing to a good degree how robust they are, and how likely it is for new vulnerabilities to be discovered in them.

Other techniques can and should still be used, but the cost of performing some of these tests drops dramatically, making them available to everyone rather than just large organizations. Further, they are repeatable, which means they can be used on different products using the same process with small to no additional infrastructure costs.

Business Pressure

Choosing software that will be up to scratch and will result in fewer losses due to security issues becomes a business concern.

Reactive vs. Proactive, and Security as Part of the Business

In today's world with increasing awareness of security threats, and security being considered a part of the business in many organizations, there is business pressure to maintain security.

Patching and similar techniques are useful, but reactive. They take time to implement, and in some cases don't work. If a product can be chosen ahead of time on the criterion that it is more robust and less likely to have vulnerabilities discovered and publicly disclosed, all the better.

With the ever-decreasing time until exploit code is released after a vulnerability becomes known, even without taking into consideration the testing and implementation time for patches, a more proactive approach is needed.

To illustrate this, even if the patching systems are perfect and all known vulnerabilities are patched, with the increase in targeted attacks using as-of-yet unknown vulnerabilities (or 0days—zerodays) to attack our organizations and executives, we cannot always rely on patches.

Saving Costs by Using Fuzzing

By using the concept of *fuzz before purchase*, you will see some benefits both short and long term, including:

- Being forced to patch less often.

- The lack of need to patch systems with no new vulnerabilities.

- Critical systems such as production servers (which patching may not even be a viable option for) would be more secure, reducing risk.

- Reducing risk of outbreaks.

- Reducing risk of targeted attacks.

- Making the window of vulnerability from exploit to patch irrelevant in more cases.

- Pressure from partners.

In recent years, organizations have been looking for a way by which they could cooperate with other organizations securely, trusting them. As testing for how secure another organization may be is difficult and at times not possible, standardization has been picked as a good indication of the other organization being security-aware and doing what needs to be done. BS7799/ISO17799 (now ISO27001 and ISO17799) proved to be good standards that many started to follow, and is a good example.

Certification by Product

Although without such standards, some organizations such as telecommunication giants and banks started demanding that vendors that want to sell to them first be tested by certain fuzzing products, with proof provided. This is far from a standard and is not a certification as such, but does show a trend.

SDL

Not for the end client, Microsoft's Software Development Lifecycle is an example of another type of pressure, although solely for vendors. SDL is the standard Microsoft pushes for secure development, and third-party development companies wishing to work on Microsoft code are required to follow it.

Fuzzing is a part of SDL, and because of that, many vendors now incorporate fuzzing into their development cycle.

Software Security Certification

With security testing becoming lower cost and more efficient, it can be expected that some type of testing rather than by the demands of partners and clients will be done.

This in turn has the potential of turning into a certification, declaring a product is built securely, and not just as a rubber stamp.

Meeting Standards and Compliance

Much like vulnerability assessment is essential in passing audits, standardization and compliance testing, the concept of *fuzz before purchase* can increase an organization's chances of passing such audits.

Proof of testing products for security before they are even implemented, and how this has made the organization's patch management system more efficient, can help your organization prove your status to auditors.

Tester Certification

With the increasing use of fuzzing in end-client organizations and corporations, a standard for how to use fuzzing will be required. Further, qualified personnel would have to be found or trained.

Certifying such personnel in training is going to become a necessity, and the role of the QA Security Engineer is born.

Industry Pressure

One could hope that when many end-client organizations test products and purchase based on how securely they are built, and report issues back to the vendor and demand them to be fixed, others will follow suit or be left behind.

Fuzzing has the potential of helping the software industry become more secure, and finally rid us of the lower hanging fruit, the simple vulnerabilities that are easy to find and keep haunting us and placing our organizations at risk.

With the maturing fuzzing industry, vendors run out of excuses to produce insecure products. Hopefully, this vision of upping the ante will be realized, but until it does, at the very least we can make sure to buy what's up to scratch, rather than deal with the added risk later.

Antivirus Product Testing and Certification

The only certification and widely deployed testing in the security industry today for vendors is for antivirus products.

These products are tested for many different things, including:

- The number of virus samples they identified
- How well these infections are removed
- The antivirus' capability to detect the virus on access

There are many concerns in testing and the resulting certification, though, which the world of security testing for products can learn from.

The main questions would be: what criteria are used for the testing, and what are the processes and environments used for the testing? What type of testing is used?

One of the biggest problems is what sample pool you would use for testing a product. This is especially important, as if you test a product with only one type of samples, it may not do as well as others.

How you determine what samples should be used for testing is another problem; after all, if the antivirus doesn't identify some "junk file" left behind by the virus, or a sample that doesn't work, it may not mean it always should.

Another concern is that once such testing is performed and made public, if one antivirus doesn't do as well as one of its competitors due to a mistake, it will take a long time for that marketing damage to be repaired.

These issues only begin to describe how problematic testing and its ramification can be. The world of security certifications for products is re-awakening, but what certification we choose to use or rely on is another question all together.

How to avoid a rubber stamp, what would be a good certification, and what damages can the certifications cause the vendor or the client, if not done correctly?

Chapter 9

What Is a File?

Solutions in this chapter:

- Are File Fuzzers Special?
- Analyzing and Building Files
- Frameworks

Introduction

Since we are interested in the fuzzing aspects, and to study generating various malformed files, we will make some distinctions first:

- A file is some sort of input for an application.

- Configuration file (could be in formats such as XML, INI)

- Data file (e.g., GIF, AVI, EML)

- We assume there must be an automated process to "generate" ("save") that file, as it was generated by some application.

- Following the same logic, we deduce there must be an automated process to "load" the file.

- The file format could be binary or textual—this would become relevant in the way we treat data inside it.

Our agenda is to provide a process to generate a large number of potentially malicious files, and have each separately tested with the application. This process would be divided to:

1. File generation/creation.

2. File load (by an external application, which we would like to test).

Next, we need to understand the difference between network protocol fuzzers and file fuzzers:

1. Generating the tests.

    a. How do we research/analyze files so our test will be built properly?

    b. How do we build the files?

2. Once a list of test cases is generated, how should we approach running the actual tests?

    a. How do we automate the process?

    b. How do we detect problems?

Are File Fuzzers Special?

When discussing network fuzzers, we looked at ways to build the actual test cases. It only makes sense that when you want to fuzz some sort of file specification, the first step would be to analyze the file and determine its structure. If this is well documented, this might be a reasonable task. We already have the file divided into sections/structure and all we have to do is wrap everything together and start altering and manipulating each section to create the list of files.

Of course, this is not enough. Even if the documentation is all there, we should try to expand our test to areas the documenters did not think of. Before diving in, we have to ask, "Is this concept any different from network fuzzing?" The answer is probably not. Once we do have our list of files to test, we have to think about how to run them. This part is obviously different from testing some server via a socket, but let's leave that for now.

So, why are file fuzzers, or more accurately *creation* of file test cases through a fuzzer, so special they deserve their own chapter? Let's think of a proprietary network protocol that has no documentation whatsoever. How would we try to research this scenario? First, we would probably set up a lab with the desired tested server installed. Next, we would hopefully find and install a few supporting clients and start simulating some actions. We can then use a sniffer to capture the data, analyze it, and learn the protocol's basic structure, according to our actions.

We can also recreate those sessions ourselves. Simply open a telnet session with the server and send the packet captures. We can play around with the packet and change parts of it to see how the server responds. The fact that we have an interactive session with the server allows us to play with the protocol and learn its structure. How could this be simulated with files? Well, let's think of a very, very, very (+very*1024) simple example first. Microsoft's Notepad (Figure 9.1) is a simple text editor that allows us to view and edit text files. Of course, this is not an interesting fuzzing example, but it's so simple that it's worth spending the time to present the concept.

Let's open Notepad and enter some text.

Figure 9.1 Microsoft's Simple Text Editor

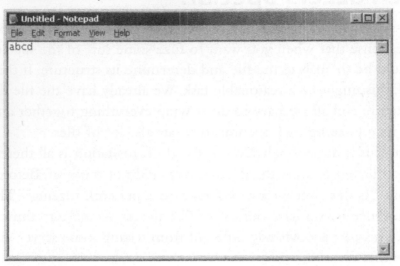

Let's save this text file.

In Notepad's Save As dialog (Figure 9.2), we see there are four types of file encoding options.

Figure 9.2 Four File Encoding Options in Notepad

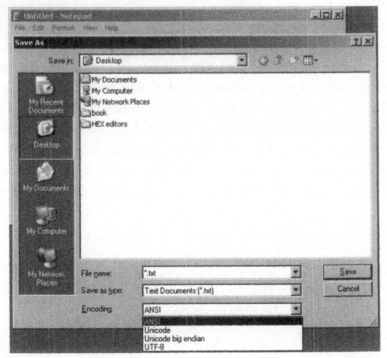

Let's save four versions of our simple text file, one for each encoding. Now, let's view the hex representation of the file (Figures 9.3 through 9.6). (Note: Re-opening in Notepad would not work, as it parses the "headers.")

Figure 9.3 ANSI

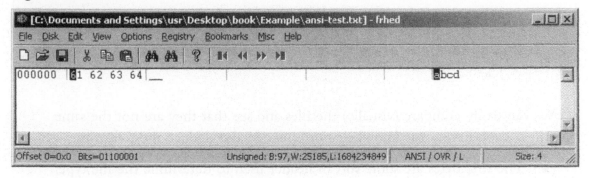

Figure 9.4 Unicode

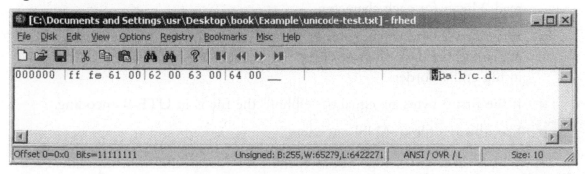

Figure 9.5 Unicode Big Endian

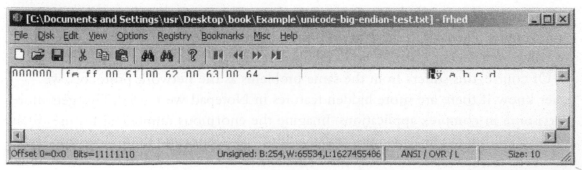

Figure 9.6 UTF-8

We can easily compare (visually) the files and see that they are not the same. We might even have some knowledge of Unicode and deduce the following:

- The first bytes are some sort of header used to determine the file type.

- If the first 2 bytes are equal to "fffe," the file encoding is Unicode. While parsing the rest of the file we would treat characters as Unicode, meaning read 2 bytes for each character.

- If the first 2 bytes are equal to "feff," the file encoding is Unicode big endian, so we parse the rest of the files reading 2 bytes for each character but in big endian order.

- If the first 3 bytes are equal to "efbbbf," the file is in UTF-8 encoding.

- Else, this is a file in ANSI encoding.

So, we have some knowledge of Notepad's TXT file specification structure. Pretty simple, and we can easily build a fuzzer to test this, adding the relevant conditions to parsing the actual text data according to the header.

This process is similar to what we explained about network fuzzers. We take a sample, play around with it, and have the "server"—in this case, the file application—generate more samples. Then, all we have to do is find the similarities and differences. Eventually, we will have a decent grasp on how the file is built.

Of course, this suffers from the same problems as the network protocols: we never know if there are more hidden features in Notepad we missed. This gets more worrisome in complex applications. Imagine the enormous number of features in an Adobe PDF file (adding pictures, tables, colors, …)—repeating the process for each and every feature seems not very time efficient…

Another problem is having the application give us some hints on how to further build a file. While sending an invalid packet to a server might respond with the problem (missing field perhaps) or a list of known commands (or in fact, sometimes there is a special command for doing just that), applications that fail to load a file would rarely report an interesting error.

Therefore, whenever we can generate file samples, we might get sufficient output to understand at least part of the file. This is a good place to start, and is reproducible for many file types (e.g., for MP3, change the bit rate, frequency, and other parameters to change the "header." Again, this is not a full solution, but a good starting point.

Now let's refer to the scenario where it is difficult to "manually" generate many file samples. With network protocols, we have the ability to capture traffic and simulate many samples in a short time. The real added value is that there are a few analyzing tools that parse the data for us and help us with analyzing (Wireshark is a good example).

Say we managed to get our hands on a satisfying list of samples to use. How can we use these to build our module? Must we manually go over and hope to understand the inner structures? While in textual files this might be a sane task, assuming most files are actually binary this seems like a lot of hard work.

Analyzing and Building Files

In this section, we suggest techniques for analyzing files and building some output from that research.

First, we need to understand the way the tested application handles this file. As it is obvious there is no point in testing a file specification by itself (how could we test this abstract concept?), we need to decide which application(s) would be used to load the file. These are the applications we would be actually testing. This process is straightforward, as we assume our main goal is testing a specific application, and the file format is simply one of the interfaces of this application (configuration file, media players, etc.).

If we are actually working on a file format intended for wide use and our goal is to check whether our spec is vulnerable, we would have to target down a few (probably well known and popular) applications that load our file type and use them for our testing process. If we provide some API or package to work with our file, we would have to test it using some simple tester application. A common way to divide the way an application handles a file is into two parts: parsing and rendering. Parsing usually takes place first, when the application is first given the file. It must load the file, read its input, and convert it into a memory structure to work with (XML elements, maps, buffers). In fact, it might be logical that the parser would be a separate library provided by some vendor and incorporated in the application, as it contains no special logic but the file format.

Rendering is the part in the application that takes the actual data inside the file and tries to work with it—display a bitmap on the screen, play a movie, update the application with the relevant settings, or anything else the application was supposed to do with this file. In some cases, parsing and rendering are mixed together—parse some data, render it, parse more date, render that, and so on. Notice that these are two different procedures in the application. Some data might be able to pass parsing but would not render (an image viewer would parse a valid in structure bitmap but refuse to show it if some parts are missing). A good example of this is looking into XML files (let's ignore XML schemes for this example):

```
<Settings Name="Example1" RequiredAttribute1="5" />
```

This line is a valid XML line and thus would pass the "parsing" process. The application then requires reading the attribute *RequiredAttribute* and using its value. This is the "rendering" part.

If we omit the *RequiredAttribute1* part and keep the line:

```
<Settings Name="Example1" />
```

this is still a valid XML, but while the "parsing" process would pass with no problems, "rendering" would painfully fail.

To summarize, we would obviously aspire to create various test cases to check both types of application procedure. To do so, we will need to generate a file that is valid and choose specific locations in the file (or combination of specific locations) to tamper with.

This chapter mostly focuses on binary files, as they present a more complicated problem. So, let's get textual files out of the way first.

Textual Files

The nice thing about textual formatted files is that by definition they are usually easier on the eye. Even before attempting to have any automatic process to analyze them, we can view them in our favorite textual editor and sometimes even read actual words that explain the meaning of each field. Even if the field's name is not clear to us, we can try to find patterns for delimiters and get a grasp on how parsing that data would work.

In addition, it is easy to use an application such as WinMerge to compare two files to distinguish between required fields and optional ones.

Another interesting thing we might want to do is detect patterns in a file. Here are some general options:

- **Find delimiters.**   Blindly go through the file and cut once a specific character is encountered. Try to visualize an HTTP Request cut in the blocks for every space/question mark/quote mark. This is not perfect, but goes a long way for us. NULL termination/new line breaks are also always popular for textual files.

- **Check for special textual patterns (with/without regular expression).** Look for all elements beginning with a specific text, containing format of "field=number."

- **Try matching conditions between two elements.**   Find all strings that are preceded with a number that equals their length.

- **Do the opposite.**   For each string, try looking up its size (as number) in the file.

Other techniques, which we discuss next, could also be adapted here.

Binary Files

This gets a bit trickier. Most binary files present the following problems:

- Unfamiliar/new data is not readable to the human eye (yes, even to those of you who feel very comfortable with 1/0s).

- As a result, comparing binary files is a less efficient task.

- When a binary file is presented, it usually means that the file is used for something more complex to begin with—a simple settings file would rarely need to be binary. Even e-mails hold the nonprintable data as textual using some encoding (Base64, Quoted Printable) and try to keep things textual.

    Binary files are used where complex structures with inner dependencies need to be stored efficiently (time and space).

- Ordinary pattern searches would not work on binary formats—we need to get smarter.

In spite of all that, binary files are not the single most troubling problem in modern science. In fact, it is probably not such a difficult and frightening task once we get a bit of experience and some tools under our belt.

So before jumping into what can be done, let's think of what would we like to be able to do:

- Analyze the file! If possible, as in Wireshark, have some parsing automatically done on the file to allow us to view the inner structures, and not the full file.

- Specifically, if exist a designated "editor"/"viewer" to our file format, we would be almost there.

- Assuming analyzing is not fully possible (meaning, no such designated editor exists), we would like to have some process/algorithm help us guess how this file is built. Again, search for patterns, but this time, smarter patterns.

- Compare the file with known file structures:

    - ASN1 (Type-Length-Value)

- Search for patterns that present a type of data, its length, and then a value at that length.

    - Length-Value

- Search for printable strings of a minimum size and divide the file around them.

Once the data is accumulated, we can easily calculate some statistics to help us decide which structure best fits our file.

- If we know our file is ASN1 compliant (or any other format, let's say it has a BNF or corresponds to a Context-Free-Grammar), we can try parsing the files using specific rules.

- Compare the file with known file formats:

    - If you know your file's format, perhaps someone already did some work for you and you can base your research on that.

    - Perhaps there is a similar file format you can compare to.

- Split the file in to smaller chunks and isolate each while researching.

- Have an automated process "hack" the tested application, check which bytes it reads from the file and how much, and give us an extensive report.

We're going to skip the magical editor/viewer part. This is rarely the case, but if we do have that special editor/viewer, our task is easy.

We have to understand that even in known, common, and popular file formats, the difference between two files could be distinctive; therefore, even in the easier cases, such an "editor" exists only for parts of the file, if at all.

Let's think back to our Notepad example. This was a very simple, but still, binary file. Well, its header was… (after all, there wasn't anything much more there).

The first tool we used to see how the file is really built was a HEX editor. While there are many HEX editors out there (some for free, some for purchase), in general this seems like our Wireshark file equivalent—it "captures" data, displays it, and as we will soon see, sometimes offers various tools to explore the file further.

In fact, HEX editors could be the answer for all our wishes, except the file sniffer.

Let's try to think more technically, and be a bit more specific with our demands:

- Ability to open a file from the disk/from memory.

- Once we recognize a pattern, look for similar patterns across the file and mark them visually (highlight them with a specific color).

- Run external scripts on the file; we want the HEX editor to allow us to write an extension that performs our proprietary tasks. Such extensions could be:

  - Comparing files

  - Merging files

  - Run statistical scripts (number occurrences of…)

  - Find regularity

  - Create grammar according to file

  - Find conditional elements within a file

- Templates support—compare to an existing set of file format templates.

- Perform complex calculations—we are working with binary/HEX data and would probably get around to calculating offsets, sizes, network/host order representation, etc.

- Script recording (macros)—re-execute a manual process.

- Change file—perhaps we can use the HEX editor to simulate test files. This could be done by running some external script that takes advantage of the editor's knowledge of structures and performs specific tasks on it:

  - Change order of data (byte swap)

  - Replace specific data with random data

  - Duplicate data

- Export to C/Perl code—a nice way to start our auto-creation process is to have some base code that already has the basic structures of the file detailed.

Now let's look at a few HEX editors and specify their main features:

010 editor—trial available (www.sweetscape.com/010editor/)

- Ability to mark and paint fields (add bookmarks to sections in a file).

- Can run external scripts such as "create random data", "isASCII?", "split files", "multiple paste", and more, which can be found at www.sweetscape.com/010editor/scripts/.

- Can be extended with your own scripts.

- Use templates to look at predefined file section (from a pre-defined list of zip, bmp, wav, and more, which can be found at www.sweetscape.com/010editor/templates/—edit and write your own.

- Ability to compare binary files.

- Advanced calculation and operations (such as bitwise operations, data format conversions).

HexProbe—evaluation available (www.hexprobe.com/index.htm)

- Allows you to set data marks (in an XML format).

- Set bookmarks inside file.

- Advanced search operations (for patterns).

- Pre-defined templates (PE, wav, ico, bmp—more can be found at www.hexprobe.com/hexprobe/template_resource.htm)

- Compare binary files.

AXE3—trial available (www.axe-editor.com/)

- Allows you to define your own structures (some included, such as PE).

- Allows you to run external scripts (isASCII? Calculate RVA, Byte swap).

- Allows setting bookmarks in file.

- Advanced compare for binary files.

- Ability to find regularities within a file.

- Ability to attempt to create grammar from a file.

- Ability to run statistical functions on a file.

Tiny Hexer (www.mirkes.de/en/freeware/tinyhex.php)

- Ability to set bookmarks within a file.

- Ability to insert part of a file into a different file.

- Ability to perform statistical functions on file data.

- Ability to compare files.

- Ability to run scripts on code such as strings, resize data, highlight, split, fill with random/calculated data, script recording (macro), and more.

- Ability to extend with your own plug-ins.

So, this can help us take a file sample and manually analyze it.

By loading the structure viewer, and using the predefined bmp template, we can easily navigate through the structures in the file and their values, and pretty much understand what should/could be changed.

Once we begin to understand our file's patterns, we can write our assumptions as a template and start comparing files using it. This would make the chore of verifying a theory much easier.

We can see that only the headers change, and the color table is the same (go back to the structure viewer to identify the exact locations). The last thing on our wish list was a "file sniffer." Since we start with some file samples, we can have the application load them.

Remember our assumption that there is an automated process to "generate" and "load" these files. Using that assumption, we could try to "record" all actions made to the file, by the application (either during load or save, each of the operations has its advantages), and then use that report data while we view the file in our editor.

An interesting data might look like this:

- 42 bytes were read from offset 12 => might suggest that this is some structure.

- 1 byte was read from offset 64 and then X bytes were read from offset 65 => might suggest this is a Length–Value structure.

This data could be collected in one of the following methods:

- Use a device driver to track file operations (such as SysInternal's FileMon). This would let us know whenever a file is opened, read from, written to, and closed.

- Use an API monitor to track file access function calls.

- Could use any existing reverse-engineering tool that allows adding breakpoints to functions (Soft-Ice, IDA, OllyDbg).

- Could use simple API monitors such as APISpy or Rohitab's API Monitor.

- Could write your own application that hooks specific functions and logs relevant parameter data.

We won't go any deeper on how to perform this, as that is a different subject that deserves its own attention. So, to summarize, it seems that these tools and features are a nice start to working with a file. However, even if we think we have the theory part figured out, we must test our data/changes to see that it is aligned with the application's behavior.

This would probably be done toward the end of the process, while running the actual test on a large amount of test files, but is also necessary during the learning process, to see whether our conclusions stand and that our generated files are somewhat valid, so they would not be thrown away by the application at first sight. This nicely leads us to our next section on how to perform the actual testing ("running") of the files.

Running the Test

A few problems still stand in our way to finding vulnerabilities in our file product. While the first, generating the samples, is out of the way, we still need to think of how to feed these test cases to our application and (of course) how to detect potential problems. As usual, let's start by seeing how this is done in network fuzzer scenarios.

Interface

- Network test cases have an obvious interface—network, and usually via a socket.

- File test cases have a similar common interface, the File->Open menu option. While it is true that in many cases it is possible to load a file using other methods, such as drag-and-dropping into the application, running the application from the command line with the filename as input, import and more, we will assume that either we would handle all of these options (preferably), or that they all bottle down to the same code and therefore one method covers them all (or at least close enough). In some cases, such as working on an application's configuration file, there is no interface to load the file. Still, something loads it. We just need to figure out how this is done and find a solution for automating that process (for example, replace the actual configuration file and start the application).

Test Flow

Network test cases sometime need to preserve a session throughout the test (e.g., Login before Commands). In addition, problems in one session might affect a following session, which might be hard to detect.

- File test cases—well, it seems we finally found something easier in file fuzzers! There doesn't seem to be "Sessions" in file format cases. In fact, most applications do not load and reload files on the fly so we may even decide to close the application entirely after each test and restart it for the next one.

    However, this requires the observation that our application is not being tested for multiple file operations. Memory leak in load would not crash the application and might not be detected until it does (which would take, let's say, 15 sequential load operations).

    Again, we make the choice to simplify this matter and treat each test on its own. If your file application is different, and cannot make this assumption, you are not left out to dry—the change is reasonable. In fact, the main difference is in parsing the error report and determining which file caused the problem. We would address this issue later.

Network errors are detected when:

- Server crashes—could be detected by a monitoring agent, such as a debugger.

- Server stops responding.

- Server reports specific error to some log file.

- Server sends specific packet back to client (someone must parse the packet and detect discrepancies.

File errors should be detected when:

- Application crashed—can be detected by attaching a debugger to the application.

- Application hangs—put a timer on an application's run, detect high memory usage and stop it, check its log size and stop it when it exceeds a certain size.

- Application reports a specific error to some log file—could be detected by parsing the log file.

- Application alerts user with a specific message (Message box, stdout/stderr, etc.).

We can see that the difference is minute, and aside from detecting an application "Reply," which is something a bit different in network fuzzers as well, the same mechanisms could be used.

Side effects:

- Network tests can be affected by several nontest-related issues:

  - Network connectivity problems (our fuzzing was so extensive and hard that we burned out the router?).

  - Due to a large number of requests, the server filled the machine with log files and took up all the free space (whether this is a potential vulnerability is debatable).

  - Once crashed, server must restart for us to resume testing.

File tests can be affected by:

- Generating our files test cases might take up all our disk space. We need to keep that in mind (either have enough disk space or generate a test-case, run, delete file test case if no problem was reported).

- Once crashed, the application might go into safe mode. Not sure this was our intent (to test following files in safe mode).

So, now that we know what we want to do, and have some ideas on how to do it, let's look at several of the file fuzzers out there. Notice that most of them try to deal with both parts of our process, meaning generating files from some source and running to detect problems.

iSEC Partners—FileP

FileP is a python-based file fuzzer. It generates mutated files from a list of source files and feeds them to an external program in batches.

This fuzzer gets a source file and an application command. It then looks for predefined patterns in the source file, changes them to a malicious pattern, and executes the application, giving the filename as a parameter.

Output is the list of files that triggered an application error (www.isecpartners.com/file_fuzzers.html).

iDefense's FileFuzz

FileFuzz is a graphical Windows-based file format fuzzing tool. It was designed to automate executing the launching of applications and detection of exceptions caused by fuzzed file formats (http://labs.idefense.com/software/fuzzing.php).

It takes a file as input, parameters to choose bytes to manipulate from and changes them. It also has default settings for various file applications/specifications (acrobat, ntbackups, zip, wmf, wab, etc.).

eEye—Integer File Fuzzer (UFuz3)

UFuz3 is a binary file fuzzer focused on finding integer overflow vulnerabilities. This tool can audit any application that loads a binary file such as Windows Media player, Microsoft office, etc. (http://research.eeye.com/html/tools/RT20070129.html).

This fuzzer gets an input file and application path and generates sample files. It then tests them with the application and reports the files that generated a crash/error. Test files are generated by searching for integer overflows patterns (supporting size, offsets, little/big endian).

Gianni's fuzzer

Given a filename and an application path, Gianni's fuzzer generates files according to patterns (predefined or tailored) and reports which files crashed the application with the relevant debug information (http://gruba.blogspot.com/2006/11/file-fuzzer.html).

zzuf

zzuf is a transparent application input fuzzer. Its purpose is to find bugs in applications by corrupting their user-contributed data. It works by intercepting file and network operations and changing random bits in the program's input (http://sam.zoy.org/zzuf/).

This takes a bit of a different approach, where it tries to generate files dynamically according to the way an application reads input files and not statically. The application needs to be "fed" with various sample files.

untidy

untidy is general-purpose XML fuzzer. It takes a string representation of an XML as input and generates a set of modified, potentially invalid XMLs based on the input (http://untidy.sourceforge.net/).

mangle.c

mangle.c is a trivial binary file fuzzer by Ilja van Sprundel.

Its usage is very simple: it takes a filename and header size as input. It will then change approximately between 0 and 10% of the header with random bytes (biased toward the highest bit set).

Frameworks

Fuzzing frameworks do not offer a "complete" solution as previous examples, but do offer you some platform to use your research data to construct an effective file generator. It is important to understand that even after we have all the technical information about our file specification, we still need to decide how to alter its structures and whether to generate files such that each has only one "broken" point or some "magic combination" of broken parts.

Fuzzled—Perl Fuzzing Framework

Offers some code to generate data and some code for generating advanced elements such as Repeated data/Format String/Filename/Unicode (and more). In addition, provides several pre-built examples, mostly for network protocols.

AntiParser

AntiParser is a fuzz testing and fault injection API (http://antiparser.sourceforge.net/).

Monitoring the Application with the Test Cases

So, we established we need to analyze a file format and generate various test files. We also know that our next step is to run and find problems.

We noticed that most file fuzzers take the same approach:

1. Analyze an input file and generate various test files:

   a. Simply by replacing data with random data

   b. More advanced—by replacing data inside specific patterns with different data

   c. By a predefined file format (which we can only assume is a result of some research)

2. Run the file on a given application with some monitoring tool.

3. And, of course, report your findings.

So, the last thing on our task list is to run the actual test.

Assume we have a directory full of potentially problematic files. We would want to run them, one after the other, and monitor the application's response.

This could be done in various ways, but the simplest is to have a script, iterating over all files in the folder and running the application.

Most file-accepting applications allow launching with a filename as a parameter. If not, we can simulate an application with any action, but this is obviously less generic.

Next, we would like to have a sanity check performed at the start of the test, feeding the application with some of the files we created and already manually checked. This would be done to make sure the testing process is valid and that the application does not simply reject all files on some minor issue.

Once this is done, we need to determine how to detect that the application finished working on a specific file. While normal/standard files might simply be a matter of waiting a few seconds and closing, large files might take more time, hang the application, or even simply alert the user with some question and wait for input.

While we cannot address any specific case or question the application might raise, we can mark these cases with some tag for us to check manually later. (We're hoping this would not be too common. If it is, we would have to find a way to handle it on our script.)

Now that these cases are marked, we can skip them and go on to the next test case. So, we have an algorithm, iterating over files, loading them into the application and exiting the application. Now we need to attach the application run to some monitoring process. Any debugger would do the trick, as long as we can handle the Exception Reports, save the malicious file, and resume the test. gdb, IDA, and OllyDbg, which provide various plug-ins, seem like good candidates.

Finally, we can add external checks for log messages, code coverage, memory/CPU usage, and other system events to check for other types of data. Our results should consist of files that caused some problem (and the relevant data found, whether this is from the debugger, the log parsing, or any other event) and suspicious files that could not be tested automatically. This allows us to dig deep into each of these suspicious scenarios by reproducing it, and by doing so, further investigate the problem to its solution.

Chapter 10

Code Coverage and Fuzzing

Solutions in this chapter:

- **Code Coverage**
- **Obtaining Code Coverage**
- **Improving Fuzzing with Code Coverage**
- **Weaknesses of Code Coverage**

- ☑ **Summary**
- ☑ **Solutions Fast Track**
- ☑ **Frequently Asked Questions**

Introduction

Many related problems arise during the fuzzing of real applications. First, some mutation-based fuzzers will run indefinitely, endlessly modifying data and supplying it to the target application. Assuming the application never crashes, how do we know when to turn off this type of fuzzer? When is enough? Another problem that arises comes after running a finite set of fuzzed test cases, such as those generated by SPIKE or supplied by a PROTOS test suite. If the target application has not crashed, and the fuzzer is finished, what do we do next? Can we call the application secure and move on? Is it possible to measure how well the application has been fuzzed? Is there a way to make "improved" test cases based on the results of previous fuzzing runs?

The answers to all these questions can be found by closer examination of the actions of the application being fuzzed. This chapter demonstrates how to use code coverage, a measure of the amount of code executed by an application, to make decisions on how successful fuzzing has been and how this information can be used to make fuzzing even more effective.

Code Coverage

Code coverage is a metric often used by software developers and testers to help determine when applications have been sufficiently tested. Typically, code coverage information is obtained by adding additional code to the application when it is built. Adding code to a binary is called *instrumenting* the code. (We'll see later that there are other ways to obtain code coverage). This additional code is responsible for recording the coverage information when the application is executed. This recorded coverage information is then post processed by another application that computes the amount of code covered, and generates reports and graphs.

There are many different types of code coverage, the most basic being *statement coverage*. This refers to whether lines in the source code have been executed. We will also extend this notion to include whether lines in assembly code have been executed, for applications in which we do not have the corresponding source code. From this information we can compute the percentage of the total lines of code executed, be it source or assembly. These numbers can be generated per application, and per module, file, class, or function. The information gained from these code coverage reports can lead us to particular regions of code that have not been executed and may require further analysis. This is the simplest and most common form of code coverage.

A slightly more informative type of code coverage is *branch coverage*. This type of coverage measures whether each branch, or conditional, has been taken. Again, we extend this to whether each conditional jump in assembly code has been taken. (Technically, this assembly version of branch coverage is equivalent to *multiple-condition coverage* in the testing field). Again, an aggregate number that indicates the percentage of possible branches that have been taken can be computed at various levels of the application.

A particular variation of branch coverage exists called *relational operation coverage*. This measures whether expressions containing relational operators (<, >, >=, <=) are exercised with boundary values. For example, in the following code segment,

```
if (x > 0)
  foo();
```

branch coverage would be obtained if during one execution x was greater than zero, and in another it was less than 0. However, this would not constitute complete relational operation coverage. For this more powerful metric to be maximized, we would also require a test case where x equals 0. This is very useful for detecting off-by-one errors, a common source of security vulnerabilities. This particular type of code coverage is not currently implemented in any tools.

The most complete type of code coverage is referred to as *path coverage*. This measures the number of paths in the control flow graph of the program that have been executed. This type of coverage is the most thorough type of coverage because it depends on every possible way through the control flow graph of the program. This requires various combinations of variables to be particular values at different times. Again, a percentage of paths can be calculated at various levels of the application.

While path coverage is the most thorough measurement of code coverage, it has many problems. One is that, when loops are considered, there may be an infinite number of paths. This difficulty is handled by only recording whether multiple loops have been executed; that is, two possible "paths" through a loop are covered depending on whether the loop was executed only once or multiple times.

Another problem with path coverage is the notion of *infeasible paths*. Consider the following code segment:

```
if( x > 0 )
  foo();
if( x < 0 )
  bar();
```

```
if( x == 0 )
  foobar();
```

There are eight possible paths through the control flow graph of this code. However, only three are feasible. Namely, the variable x cannot at the same time be greater *and* less than zero, so it is not possible to have both foo() and bar() called in the same execution of this code.

The most serious problem with path coverage is the exponential number of paths in an application. For instance, if a portion of a program has n total conditionals, there will be $2n$ possible branches, but 2^n possible paths. This can be seen by examining the previous code that contains three branches but has $2^3 = 8$ possible paths.

Tools & Traps...

Why One Form of Code Coverage Is More Thorough Than Others

Most code coverage tools supply statement coverage information. This can be very useful for us, but does have some limitations. Consider the following code segment:

```
if( x > 0 )
  size += x;
if( y > 0 )
  size +=y;
foo(size);
```

Suppose that upon examining the code coverage data, it is found that all statements have been executed. Have we done all we can do? Not necessarily. For example, this code segment can have complete statement coverage with only one execution (namely, when x and y are both greater than zero). However, it will require two executions to obtain total branch coverage (where x and y are both greater and less than zero, respectively). To obtain perfect path coverage, four executions are required. This demonstrates the additional information obtained by examining path coverage versus branch coverage, or branch coverage versus statement coverage, for it may be that a vulnerability only emerges down one particular path in a program.

Obtaining Code Coverage

In general, there are a few ways in which code coverage information can be collected from an application. The traditional way is to instrument the binary during compilation. Additional code is added to the compiled program, which records execution of the binary. Other ways to obtain code coverage information include injecting this additional code into a running application. Yet another option includes monitoring the target program with a specialized debugging program or simulating its execution. Let's start with the simplest example and assume we have source code.

Instrumenting the Binary

Let us examine how to use the GNU compiler gcc to obtain code coverage information for applications for which we have source code. We compile a simple program with the -fprofile-arcs and -ftest-coverage flags, which inform the compiler to add code coverage instrumentation. The following assembly code fragment from this binary illustrates the added instructions that record code coverage information. The relevant lines that record this information are highlighted.

```
0x00001b9e    <main+0>:      push    ebp
0x00001b9f    <main+1>:      mov     ebp,esp
0x00001ba1    <main+3>:      push    ebx
0x00001ba2    <main+4>:      sub     esp,0x14
0x00001ba5    <main+7>:      call    0x2ffc <__i686.get_pc_thunk.bx>
0x00001baa    <main+12>:     cmp     DWORD PTR [ebp+8],0x2
0x00001bae    <main+16>:     jle     0x1bc6 <main+40>
0x00001bb0    <main+18>:     mov     DWORD PTR [ebp-12],0x1
0x00001bb7    <main+25>:     lea     eax,[ebx+0x14de]
0x00001bbd    <main+31>:     add     DWORD PTR [eax],0x1
0x00001bc0    <main+34>:     adc     DWORD PTR [eax+4],0x0
0x00001bc4    <main+38>:     jmp     0x1bdd <main+63>
0x00001bc6    <main+40>:     mov     DWORD PTR [ebp-12],0x2
0x00001bcd    <main+47>:     lea     eax,[ebx+0x14de]
0x00001bd3    <main+53>:     lea     eax,[eax+8]
0x00001bd6    <main+56>:     add     DWORD PTR [eax],0x1
0x00001bd9    <main+59>:     adc     DWORD PTR [eax+4],0x0
0x00001bdd    <main+63>:     mov     eax,DWORD PTR [ebp-12]
0x00001be0    <main+66>:     add     esp,0x14
0x00001be3    <main+69>:     pop     ebx
0x00001be4    <main+70>:     pop     ebp
0x00001be5    <main+71>:     ret
```

An analysis of the highlighted assembly reveals a global array located at `ebx+0x14de` consisting of two 64-bit elements. These two elements are incremented every time their respective basic branch is executed. Although it's not seen here, this collected data is then dumped to the corresponding files upon a call to `gcov_exit`. Additionally, during compilation, for each source file, a file with a GCNO extension is created. This file contains information about the control flow graph of the program, and records the name of the file and functions among other things. When the program is actually executed, an additional file is created for each source file, this time with a GCDA extension. These data files can then be read by post processing programs such as *gcov* or *lcov*. Let's follow a complete example to see how this process works.

```
charlie-millers-computer:~ cmiller$ more test3.c
int main(int argc, char *argv[]){
  int ret;
  if(argc >2)
    ret = 1;
  else
    ret = 2;
  return ret;
}
charlie-millers-computer:~ cmiller$ gcc -g -fprofile-arcs -ftest-coverage -o test3
test3.c
charlie-millers-computer:~ cmiller$ ./test3
charlie-millers-computer:~ cmiller$ gcov test3.c
File 'test3.c'
Lines executed:80.00% of 5
test3.c:creating 'test3.c.gcov'
charlie-millers-computer:~ cmiller$ more test3.c.gcov
  -:0:Source:test3.c
  -:0:Graph:test3.gcno
  -:0:Data:test3.gcda
  -:0:Runs:1
  -:0:Programs:1
  1:1:int main(int argc, char *argv[]){
  -:2:int ret;
      1:   3:  if(argc >2)
  #####:  4:          ret = 1;
      :   5:  else
```

```
1:   6:         ret = 2;
1:   7: return ret;
-:   8:}
```

First, we list the contents of the file, test3.c. Next, we compile it using gcc with the appropriate flags. Then we run the program. After running it, we execute the gcov program on the source file. This reads the GCDA file, computes code coverage statistics, and generates a file named test3.c.gcov. Finally, we examine this file and observe the code coverage obtained.

Observe that executing test3 with no arguments executes 80% of the five lines. The test3.c.gcov file shows that each line was executed once with the exception of line 4, which was never executed. If we wished to have 100% code coverage, we would know that we needed to make argc greater than two, although this is a trivial example.

TIP

To get branch coverage, use the –b option to gcov. This generates additional summary information, like

```
Lines executed:80.00% of 5
Branches executed:100.00% of 2
Taken at least once:50.00% of 2
No calls
```

and the GCOV file contains branch information, such as

```
2:   3:       if(argc >2)
branch 0 taken 0% (fallthrough)
branch 1 taken 100%
```

Monitoring a Closed Source Application

When we have source code, instrumenting a program to include code coverage information is as easy as adding a couple flags at compile time. Things are a little more difficult when we don't have the source code and need to get coverage data from a proprietary, closed source application. The most effective way to approach this problem is to use the open source PaiMei framework.

PaiMei (http://paimei.openrce.org/) is a reverse engineering framework that contains many useful modules. One of the modules, PAIMEIpstalker, can record and export code coverage data. It does this by attaching to the target process as a debugger, setting breakpoints at the beginning of each basic block or function, and recording when each breakpoint is hit into a MySQL database. This data is then accessible through the PaiMei GUI or may be exported to a file (Figure 10.1).

To use PAIMEIpstalker, the locations of all the basic blocks need to be identified. This is done with the help of IDA Pro (datarescue.com/idabase/index.html), a commercial disassembler. By using a special file developed for use in IDA Pro, these values can be exported into a file with the extension PIDA. (Please see the PaiMei site for more instructions on how to use the framework and this module.) Once this PIDA file is input into PAIMEIpstalker, and the command to begin stalking is issued, each time a breakpoint is hit, it is stored in memory. Upon completion, this information is exported into a MySQL database and can additionally be exported into a file that can be imported back into IDA Pro to highlight those instructions that have been executed. More details are shown in the next section when we carry out this procedure with an example.

Figure 10.1 PaiMei Console

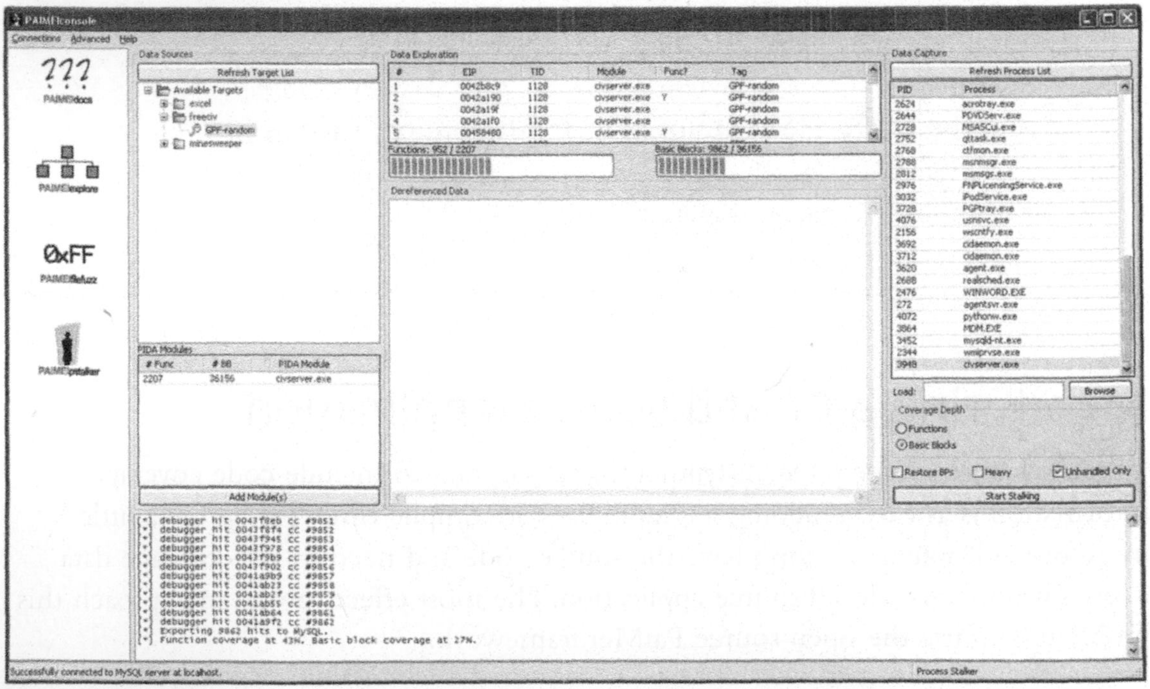

Tools & Traps...

Code Coverage for Other Languages

We've only been discussing code coverage with respect to C/C++ source code and x86 binaries, but the concept can be applied to any language or architecture. In fact, there are code coverage tools available for most popular languages. For example, EMMA and JCover can be used for Java code. NCover is a code coverage tool for .NET, coverage.py for Python, and Devel::Cover for Perl.

A commercial tool exists, Fortify Tracer, from Fortify Software, designed especially to provide code coverage for Web applications.

Improving Fuzzing with Code Coverage

Thus far, we've talked about what code coverage is and how to get it. Now we will see how to use this information to evaluate and improve fuzzing. We do this via an example.

We will consider the Freeciv (freeciv.org) open source game that comes with many Linux systems. This game comes with a server that manages the game play and a client all the players use to connect to the server and interact with one another. This is a great example for fuzzing because

- The client and server communicate with an undocumented protocol.

- The protocol is binary based.

- The code is buggy as hell.

The first thing we need to do is enable the collection of code coverage. To do this we need to compile and instrument the code such that code coverage will be recorded. We simply run

```
CFLAGS="-g -fprofile-arcs -ftest-coverage" ./configure
make
```

This will build the program with the added instructions to record code coverage, as we discussed earlier. You can verify this is correct by verifying the existence of corresponding GCNO files. Next, start the server:

```
./bin/civserver
```

At this point, we can commence fuzzing the server. For this example, we'll use the General Purpose Fuzzer (GPF) (appliedsec.com/resources.html) in "main" mode. In this mode, valid traffic is first captured by the user and then GPF resends the traffic while injecting faults into the traffic (i.e., adding randomness to the existing captured traffic). This should have the advantage that the data is closer to valid data than pure random and so should delve deeper into the application. To use this fuzzing technique, we first need to capture a valid exchange between a legitimate Freeciv client and server. We can easily do this using *tcpdump* or *Ethereal*. Next, we convert this PCAP file into one GPF understands:

```
./GPF -C freeciv_reg_game.pcap freeciv_reg_game.gpf
```

Finally, we start up GPF:

```
./GPF -G l ../freeciv_reg_game.gpf client <IP ADDRESS> 5555 ? TCP
kj3874jff 1000 0 + 0 + 00 01 09 43 close 0 1 auto none
```

This particular mode of GPF takes each packet sent from the client to the server in the full traffic capture and replaces it with random data. It repeats this 10 times for each packet. After the fuzzer finishes, let's see what kind of code coverage was obtained. Quit out of *civserver* so that the coverage data is saved. This should generate a number of GCDA files. We use lcov (http://ltp.sourceforge.net/coverage/lcov.php) to collect and display this collected data,

```
lcov -t "freeciv" -directory . -c -o freeciv-main-random.info
```

This command gathers all the code coverage information and stores it in one central file, freeciv-main-random.info. This command needs to be run from the main Freeciv directory. Finally, we run the genhtml command, a part of the *lcov* package.

```
genhtml -o freeciv-main-random -f freeciv-main-random.info
```

This creates a set of HTML documents that describe the code that was covered while fuzzing with GPF. Opening the index.html file reveals the document shown in Figure 10.2.

Figure 10.2 lcov Code Coverage Report for Initial Fuzz Run of `freeciv`

This fuzzing has executed 2373 lines, which is 5.4% of possible code, mostly in the common directory.

Without this code coverage information, we might have believed we had thoroughly tested this application. However, at this point it is clear that our fuzzing has been insufficient for this application and needs to be improved. We need test cases that will reach the large portion of lines that have not been covered. There are a few ways we can devise new test cases that will improve the code coverage.

It should also be pointed out that this code coverage information can be helpful during static analysis. We can use it to observe which lines have been executed and which lines have not. This helps in determining whether we can get data to various suspicious functions. Dynamic analysis can help static analysis, which can then help dynamic analysis, as we'll see in the following sections.

Notes from the Underground...

Take the Path Less Traveled

Years ago, a very wise man once said, "If you don't know what it does, it gives you root." He was referring to auditing daemons that run on operating systems and was pointing out that the ones that no one uses are the ones most likely to have bugs.

This same thought applies directly to fuzzing and code coverage. Namely, the code that is rarely executed and isn't covered during most testing or fuzzing, is the code most likely to have problems.

Manual Improvements

The simplest, but most time-intensive technique is to try to improve code coverage "by hand." By examining the source code in the HTML generated by *lcov*, along with the dynamic information annotated in it, it is possible to identify branches that were not taken and identify the changes locally that would have made that alternative branch to have been taken. This information can then be traced back to the input to the program and the appropriate change can be made to the test case. This can then be done for many branches, concentrating on ones that lead to new, unexplored sections of code. An example will illustrate this idea.

It makes sense to start where the user input enters the program. In this case, this will be where our network traffic is initially read. Looking through the source code, shortly after our data is read, the processing proceeds to a large switch statement, with 228 cases:

```
void *get_packet_from_connection_helper(struct connection *pc,
enum packet_type type)
{
  switch(type) {
```

This function is called from `get_packet_from_connection()`. Pulling out important portions of this function we see

```
dio_get_uint16(&din, &len_read);
whole_packet_len = len_read;
...
```

```
dio_get_uint8(&din, &utype.itype);
...

return get_packet_from_connection_helper(pc, utype.type);
```

From this, we see that the first two bytes of our data should correspond to the length of the packet, and the third byte indicates the type of the packet and is the value that is used in the large switch statement. Only a few cases of this switch statement have been executed with our fuzzing thus far (Figure 10.3).

Figure 10.3 lcov Code Coverage Report for `get_packet_from_connection_helper()` Function

Therefore, it is clear; we need to fuzz this application while varying the third byte through all possibilities to exercise more code. Again, we can use GPF to accomplish this goal. In a real audit, we would probably switch to a custom fuzzer or at least provide additional information to GPF to help it understand the protocol.

To see if we can improve the code coverage from the first run, we must clear out coverage data from the previous run.

```
lcov -directory . -z
```

Then we start up the Freeciv server and turn on GPF.

```
./GPF -G 1 ../freeciv_reg_game.gpf client <IP ADDRESS> 5555 ? TCP
kj3874jff 1000 0 + 2 10 00 01 255 41 finish 0 1 auto none
```

This replaces the bytes 2 through 10 of each packet, one at a time, with all possible values from 0 to 255. This will ensure that all the cases in the switch statement are hit. The code coverage from this run of GPF is about three times as good (Figure 10.4).

Figure 10.4 Improved lcov Code Coverage Report after More Directed Fuzzing

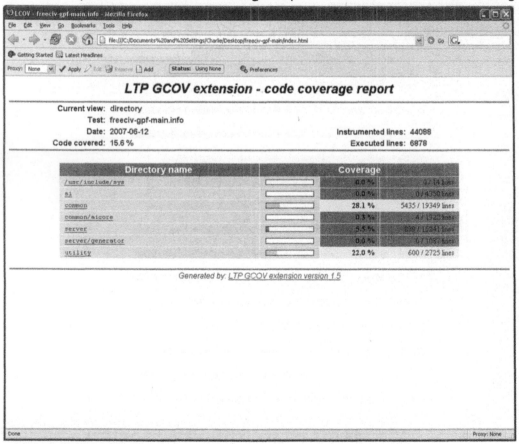

We now have 15.6% code coverage, having tripled our coverage with only one small variation in our fuzzing. Also, as we predicted, we hit every case in that switch statement. This corresponds to at least a couple of hundred additional processing functions we have hit.

However, we are still only at 15.6% coverage. What is the next step? As before, we need to manually identify portions of code that haven't been executed yet, and try to design our future test cases such that they will be executed. We should especially concentrate on portions of code that haven't been exercised that contain data copying and manipulation, as these could lead to memory corruption errors. It would make sense to start going through the 228 processing functions and see how we can improve the coverage in those functions; that is, try to understand more of the protocol beyond the first 3 bytes. For the sake of brevity, we'll choose one particular packet type for closer inspection, PACKET_PLAYER_ATTRIBUTE_CHUNK. When this type of packet is processed, the function `receive_packet_player_attribute_chunk()` is called, which is a wrapper for `receive_packet_player_attribute_chunk_100()`. Examining the code coverage for this function reveals some interesting branches that were never taken (Figure 10.5).

Figure 10.5 lcov Code Coverage Report Indicating Some Missed Branches

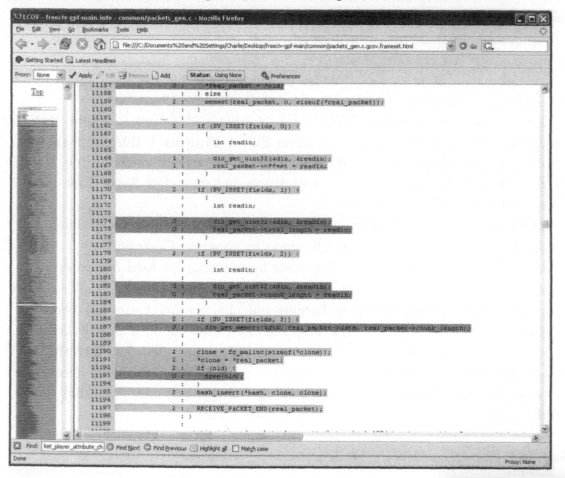

Looking at line 11187 in this source file, we see a call to `dio_get_memory()`, which is never executed. Referencing this function reveals

```
void dio_get_memory(struct data_in *din, void *dest, size_t dest_size)
{
  if (enough_data(din, dest_size)) {
    if (dest) {
      memcpy(dest, ADD_TO_POINTER(din->src, din->current), dest_size);
    }
  din->current += dest_size;
  }
}
```

so that `dio_get_memory()` is just a `memcpy()` wrapper. Therefore, looking at the code, we notice that we control the value `real_packet->chunk_length`, processed from our packet in line 11182 and elsewhere in the code we see that we control the size of the `real_packet->data` heap buffer. This leads to a classic heap overflow, found from fuzzing with the help of some information provided by the code coverage.

Of course, we won't always have source code, and hence, we won't always be able to use *gcov* and *lcov*. However, the exact same code coverage increasing procedure can be carried out for binaries using PaiMei. To demonstrate this, we outline how to do the same steps we did on the Windows binary download of Freeciv.

First, we need to generate a PIDA file. To do this, load civserver.exe into IDA Pro and allow it to finish its analysis. Then select **Edit | Plugins | IDA python**, and choose **pida_dump.py**. When prompted, indicate we want to analyze at the basic blocks level. Choose **yes** for the next two dialogs and then click **Save**. After some time, the PIDA file will be produced.

Next, start up PaiMei and select the icon for the PAIMEIpstalker module. Establish a connection to your MySQL server by choosing **Connections | MySQL Connect**. Next, load the new PIDA module by selecting the **Add Module(s)** button. Notice that there are 2207 functions and 36156 basic blocks. Prepare for the fuzzing by right clicking **Available Targets** and adding a target named Freeciv. Right click this new tag, select **Add Tag**, and call it GPF-random. Right click this new tag and **Use For Stalking**. Start up civserver.exe, and click the **Refresh Process List** button. Find civserver.exe on the list and click on it. Then choose the Coverage Depth of **Basic Blocks**, uncheck the **Heavy** box, and click **Start Stalking**. That is a lot of button pushing, but it's worth it!

Now fuzz the server as before using GPF. When GPF is finished, click **Stop Stalking**. The data will be exported to the MySQL database. To display the progress we've made, right click the **GPF-random** tag and pick **Load Hits**. This will fill in the PaiMei GUI with the code coverage information, as can be seen in the top portion of Figure 10.6. The final step is to export the data in a form we can load into IDA Pro. To do this, right click the **GPF-random** tag and select **Export to IDA**.

Finally, go back to IDA Pro, choose **File | IDC File...**, and select the file containing the exported data. After the IDC file is run, all the basic blocks that were executed during the fuzzing are colored. This helps to quickly find portions of the code that remain untested in exactly the same way as when we had the source code. Figure 10.6 shows the switch statement we identified during the packet processing, as viewed in graph mode of IDA Pro. As we can see, again, the original fuzzing did not execute many of the case statements.

Figure 10.6 IDA Pro screenshot of code coverage. The few executed basic blocks are shaded green

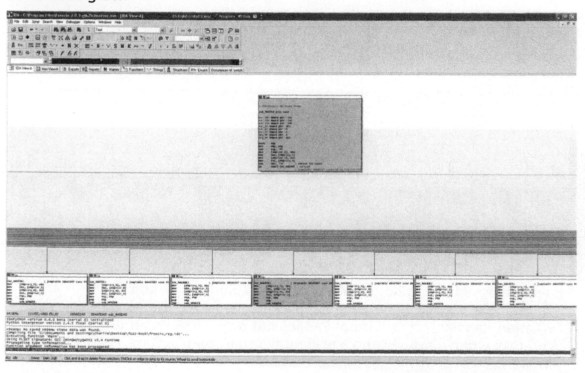

There are only a handful of basic blocks, represented as squares, that are colored green (i.e., have been executed). If we rerun GPF again, changing the bytes one at a time as we did earlier, you can see we successfully fuzz all these statements, as every basic block has been shaded (Figure 10.7).

Figure 10.7 IDA Pro Screenshot Showing All Basic Blocks in This Function Have Now Been Executed

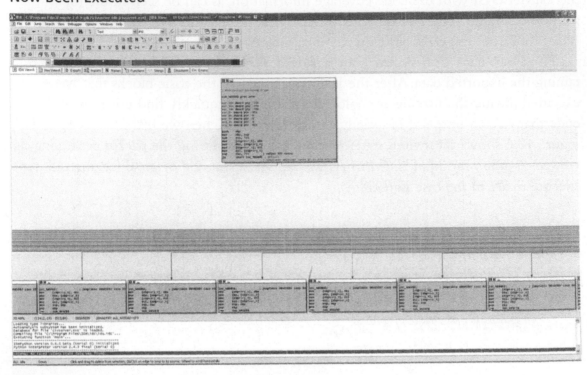

Tools & Traps...

Dealing with PaiMei Problems

Sometimes when using PaiMei's pstalker module, problems will arise. For example, we may find that our application being monitored crashes. In this situation, the likely culprit is not PaiMei, but rather IDA Pro. If IDA Pro makes a mistake when disassembling and identifies some data as code, PaiMei will set software breakpoints in that data. These changes to the data may cause the program to crash. To solve this problem, consider tuning IDA Pro to be less aggressive in its disassembly.

Another potential problem is that exceptions are occurring in the program (by design) and you have told PaiMei to catch these. In this case, ensure that the **unhandled only** box in the PaiMei GUI is checked.

A final problem that comes up is that the target application has some anti-debugging features enabled. PaiMei has some very simple mechanisms to avoid this, but will be stymied by more advanced anti-debugging features, such as those found in Adobe Acrobat Reader 8.1. In this case, some research will be required to figure out how to get PaiMei working against a particular application.

Dynamically Generating Code Coverage Improvements

While it is easy to identify portions of code that have not been executed using the previous techniques, it is incredibly time consuming, so much so that it is perhaps no faster than doing standard static analysis. Therefore, we need ways to automatically take code coverage information and use it to generate better test cases.

The first attempt at this method was by autodafe (http://autodafe.sourceforge.net/). This tool requires a description of a protocol, for which it then marks the various fields. A debugger attached to the target process then monitors "dangerous" function calls for marked data. If it observes marked data being used in one of the suspicious function calls, it increases the weight of this data; that is, this data is fuzzed with a higher priority and more thoroughly. This tool was the first to use information from the execution of a program to improve future test cases. It does have some major drawbacks, not the least of which is identifying all the dangerous functions.

We take a look at a more generic version of this idea by examining the Evolutionary Fuzzing System (EFS), which uses methods from machine learning to try to increase code coverage. Before we can understand how EFS works, we need to understand the basics of genetic algorithms (GA), as this is what EFS uses to try to generate better test cases. GAs are a technique to find approximate solutions to optimization and search problems. In our case, we're trying to find test cases that maximize code coverage. On the surface, this sounds like a perfect fit. The unique thing about GAs is that they are inspired by evolutionary biology. The optimization problem is phrased in terms of a species of organisms trying to become the most fit and survive. In our case, the test cases are the organisms and the most fit ones are the ones that obtain the most code coverage. The best thing about this approach is that the test cases get to have sex with one another!

To use GAs, we need to start with an initial population. Then, we need a way to measure an individual member of the population's fitness (i.e., via a fitness function). We also need to define how organisms in a generation are selected to breed new organisms for the next generation. Next, we need to define how organisms reproduce, through two operations—recombination and mutation. Recombination requires two organisms (wink, wink), while mutation needs only one. Finally, we need to select a point to terminate the process. Let's define these biological processes in terms of test cases and fuzzing.

First, we need our initial population. EFS has the capability to start from various seed files, which help the algorithm get started with test cases and describe some of the structure of the protocol. As a true test, we will assume no special knowledge of the protocol and start with random test cases. This could be modified in the future, of course.

Next, we need a measure of a test case's fitness. EFS uses the fitness function of how many functions (or basic blocks) were executed by a given test case. Actually, EFS measures fitness in a slightly more complicated fashion, using "pools" of test cases, but this is close enough for the sake of discussion.

For the selection of organisms for breeding, EFS favors selecting those test cases that are most fit. In fact, 70% of the time, it selects test cases from the top-half of most fit test cases. The remaining 30% of the time, it selects a test case from the entire pool.

Next, we need a way to create new test cases from existing ones, using recombination and mutation methods. For recombination of two test cases, a point is selected randomly within both test cases, the *crossover point*. Basically, the second portion of the second test case is concatenated to the first portion of the first test case, and vice versa. However, some care is taken by EFS to respect any "tokens" that it may have found in the protocol, such as carriage returns, nulls, etc. For mutation, a portion of the test case is mutated with some fixed probability. In this case, the data is replaced with fuzzing heuristics, such as long strings of As or with format string characters. Again, if the protocol is tokenized, the mutation mutates the data respecting these tokens. For termination, EFS runs for a set number of generations.

Tools & Traps...

More Genetic Algorithm Features

We've only discussed the very basics of GAs. Many other features can have a large impact on a GA's effectiveness and performance, and EFS uses some of these, including:

- **Elitism**   The most fit individual passes to the next generation unmodified.

- **Niching**   Those individuals that are dramatically different from the most fit individuals will be selected for breeding with a higher probability. This helps increase *diversity*.

- **Pooling**   Sets of individuals are considered as a whole and their total fitness is used. Pools of individuals are selected for additional breeding. In EFS, this is used because the author comments that a pool of lower fit test cases may be better at finding bugs than a single high fit test case.

Now that we have a basic understanding of genetic algorithms and how EFS uses them to try to generate new test cases, let's see it in action against our old friend Freeciv (Figure 10.8).

Figure 10.8 EFS Console

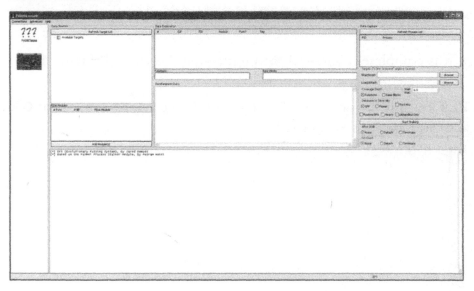

Since EFS is built on top of a modified PaiMei, we still need a PIDA file. To use EFS, first select the EFS icon on the left side of the modified PaiMei console. As in PaiMei, connect to the MySQL database by selecting **Connections | MySQL Connect**. Next, press the **Add Module(s)** button and load the corresponding PIDA file. Enter the full pathname to the civserver.exe application in the Load/Attach window. Finally, start the EFS listener by choosing **Connections | Fuzzer Connect**, followed by clicking the **Listen** button in the dialog that appears. At this point we are ready to begin fuzzing. On a client system with GPF installed, execute

```
./GPF -E <IP ADDRESS> root <PASSWORD> 0 0 <IP ADDRESS> 31338 funcs
client <IP ADDRESS> 5555 ? TCP 800000 20 low AUTO 4 25 Fixed 10 Fixed 10
Fixed 35 3 5 9 none none no
```

This tells GPF to begin evolutionary fuzzing from a random initial population ("no"), and to terminate after 35 generations. The output looks something like:

```
Successfully played generation 0. Saving to mysqldb.
Processing Generation 0 …
Done processing. Time to play and process: 100 total evaluations in
1001 seconds.
10.01 sec/eval
That's 16.683mins or 0.278hrs.
Successfully played generation 1. Saving to mysqldb.
Processing Generation 1 …
Done processing. Time to play and process: 200 total evaluations in
1887 seconds.
9.44 sec/eval
That's 31.450mins or 0.524hrs.
```

When it is complete, a graph of the progress can be viewed (Figure 10.9).

Figure 10.9 Output Graph from EFS Indicating Some Improvements of Code Coverage as Generations Progressed

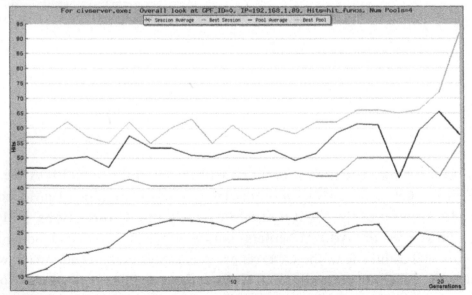

Following the light-blue line in the graph reveals that the best pool of test cases did indeed improve over these 22 generations.

This tool is still extremely experimental and holds great promise. However, it, and any GA-based technique, suffers from some inherent problems. In particular, GAs can get "stuck" at local maxima; that is to say, they get to a point where they can't increase their fitness without first greatly reducing their fitness. If you watch closely the errors generated when fuzzing Freeciv with EFS, this becomes apparent. The error messages indicate that it spends a large amount of time fuzzing the "uncompressor" routines, when it should probably be focusing on the packet type processing routines we looked at in the last section. This is another case of the human mind being smarter than the computer. Another problem with GAs is that there are so many parameters (size of population, number of pools, number of individuals per pool, length of experiment, initial population, mutation probability, etc.), it is unclear how to optimize the GA. While GA-based techniques offer an avenue to generate new test cases by searching for approximate solutions to a problem, the next section shows there may be a way to find exact solutions analytically.

Statically Generating Code Coverage

The final way to generate test cases that produce maximal code coverage is to statically examine the executable. Basically, this is the automated version of what we did manually two sections earlier. This technique is extremely cutting edge, and no available existing tool does this. Microsoft Research (ftp://ftp.research.microsoft.com/pub/tr/TR-2007-58. pdf) has an experimental tool that uses exactly this method. Catchcov (http://sourceforge. net/projects/catchconv), built upon the Linux Valgrind tool, uses similar techniques to not generate test cases, but attempt to find integer overflow errors. Since no available tool actually uses this idea to generate test cases, we'll describe how such a tool would work and some of the components that would be necessary.

To take a binary and generate a set of test cases that maximize code coverage, a few primary tasks need to be accomplished. First, the places where user-supplied data enters the application need to be identified. This data needs to be traced through the application, and each branch that is encountered needs to be recorded. Finally, we need to take the recorded information and then generate input that would take the application down different branches. This is best seen in an example. Consider the following simple C program.

```
int test(int x){
  if(x < 10){
```

```
    if(x > 0){
      return 1;
    }
  }
  return 0;
}
int main(int argc, char *argv[]){
  int x = atoi(argv[1]);
  return test(x);
}
```

Input comes into this simple program via the arguments `argc` and `argv`. Tracing through the program reveals that there is only one path through the main function. The `argv[1]` is converted into an integer and passed to the `test` function. Here, there are two branch points that depend on the argument, and different paths are executed for the following constraints on the argument:

- x >= 10
- 0 < x < 10
- x <= 0

A tool that would automatically generate test cases would need to first automatically follow the flow of the program and observe that the branch points in this function depend on the input supplied in the first argument to the program.

Now that we know the constraints on the inputs needed to achieve all three paths through the program, all that remains is finding inputs that satisfy these constraints. In this case it is obvious, but let's see how we'd do this in general for large complicated systems of constraints. To solve these equations, we need a program that can solve these types of constraints. One such program is STP (http://theory.stanford.edu /~vganesh/stp.html), a Boolean satisfiability problem (SAT) solver.

To use this SAT solver, the constraints must be expressed as a series of:

- Bit vector variables or arrays
- Word level functions, such as left and right shifts
- Bitwise operators, such as bitwise AND, OR, and XOR
- Arithmetic functions, such as add, subtract, and multiply
- Predicates, such as equal, less than, greater than

Expressing the constraints of this program in the language of STP, there are three sets of constraints to solve:

```
x : BITVECTOR(32);
QUERY(BVLT(x,0hex0000000a));

x : BITVECTOR(32);
ASSERT(BVLT(x,0hex0000000a));
QUERY(BVGT(x,0hex00000000));

x : BITVECTOR(32);
ASSERT(BVLT(x,0hex0000000a));
QUERY(BVLE(x,0hex00000000));
```

Each of these sets of constraints starts by defining the variable x as a 32-bit quantity. Then, using the predicates *BVLT*, *BVGT*, and *BVLE* (Bit Vector Less Than, Bit Vector Greater Than, Bit Vector Less than or Equal), we express the constraints on the variable x in terms of the program. Solving these equations using the SAT solver gives three inputs that maximize code coverage. To do this, we put each constraint into a separate file named *q1, q2,* and *q3,* respectively.

```
[cmiller@linuxbox stp]$ ./stp -p q1
Invalid.
ASSERT( x = 0hex0000000C );
[cmiller@linuxbox stp]$ ./stp -p q2
Invalid.
ASSERT( x = 0hex00000000 );
[cmiller@linuxbox stp]$ ./stp -p q3
Invalid.
ASSERT( x = 0hex00000004 );
```

Three inputs are discovered—0, 4, and 12—which when input as the argument to this program achieve maximal path coverage. Using this technique, very sophisticated sets of constraints, including those that would have found the path to the vulnerability discovered by hand in the Freeciv example, can possibly be solved to generate test cases from the inputs. In general, solving these constraints is not always possible, so there will be some paths for which we will not be able to find inputs to transverse.

Using this technique, these test cases can be produced without ever executing the program. Combining analytic and static approaches to fuzzing can only help to find vulnerabilities and make software even more secure.

Weaknesses of Code Coverage

Code coverage information does an excellent job of identifying parts of the application that have not been fuzzed. However, code coverage reports do not always tell the whole story when evaluating fuzzing. To illustrate this point, consider the simple function

```
mySafeCpy(char *dst, char* src){
  if(dst && src)
    strcpy(dst, src);
}
```

It is clear that code coverage could indicate that this function had been fully covered without identifying the vulnerability that is possibly present. In particular, it is not so important that this function is *executed*, which is what code coverage measures, but rather whether this function is *fuzzed*. Unless it is executed with a variety of inputs, it is possible that the vulnerability would remain hidden, despite a perfect code coverage report.

As another, more concrete example of the failure of code coverage in this regard, consider the Freeciv server example we examined earlier. We could have fuzzed Freeciv using GPF in random mode (-R), which just sends strings of random data to the server. It turns out that after about 10,000 packets, all the cases in the switch statement we explored earlier get executed under this fuzz test, although only a couple of times each. This may lead us to believe that this portion of the code was fuzzed with great detail, although it has not been. Even worse, the vulnerable lines in the `receive_packet_player_attribute_chunk_100()` function all get executed but the vulnerability is not exposed! While code coverage information is a tool that can help us improve the quality of our test cases, good code coverage does not necessarily imply good test cases.

Another problem with focusing on code coverage numbers is that it is usually impossible to execute anywhere near 100% of the code in an application. Frequently, error-checking code will not be executed except in extraordinary circumstances. For example, in the code

```
ptr = malloc(sizeof(blah));
if(!ptr)
  ran_out_of_memory();
```

the line (or branch) containing the `ran_out_of_memory()` function will not typically be executed, regardless of the fuzzing taking place. However, the fact that this line is not executed is not necessarily indicative that more fuzzing is required.

From the perspective of an attacker, the preceding problem is amplified. Consider the situation where we fuzz the Apache Web server, for example. The fuzzing will consist of making numerous HTTP requests to the server. After fuzzing is complete, we look at the code coverage and observe that we have only covered 15% of the code. What happened? Well, there will be large portions of the application over which our fuzzing has no control. For example, when the server starts up and reads its configuration file, when it is calculating how many child processes to generate based on traffic load, etc. These portions of the code may be executed, but they will certainly not be fuzzed and so we shouldn't expect complete code coverage. Even if we did find a bug in the way Apache reads its configuration files, this probably wouldn't be helpful to an attacker. Likewise, some portion of the code will not be accessible due to the configuration of the server. For example, the server may have no files protected with .htaccess files, which implies that we cannot fuzz the portion of the code that handles basic authentication. Of course, this is completely out of our control. The portion of the application that could possibly be reached from user interaction is called the *attack surface* of the application. What we are really interested in when examining code coverage while fuzzing is the amount of the attack surface that has been covered, not the total code coverage. However, it is a nontrivial task to compute this metric and no available tools do so.

Summary

Code coverage is a measure of how much of an application has been executed by testing or fuzzing. This information can be obtained by modifying the build environment to include additional instructions in the binary. It can also be obtained by monitoring a binary within a debugger and recording each function or basic block executed. While there are many different types of code coverage, most tools produce statement or branch coverage, although path coverage contains more information.

Code coverage is a valuable tool that can be used to measure the effectiveness of fuzzing. It can be used to identify portions of the application that have not been fuzzed. Additional test cases can be generated, either by hand, or automatically, to increase the effectiveness of fuzzing. The code coverage information can also be used to increase the utility of static analysis by allowing us to focus on the portions of code that have not been thoroughly tested.

While code coverage helps us find parts of the application that require additional fuzzing, achieving a high coverage rate simply means that a lot of code was executed. It does not necessarily imply that code was exercised well. After all, the point of fuzzing is to send invalid data, and valid data can generate high test coverage.

Solutions Fast Track

Code Coverage

☑ Code coverage is a mechanism that identifies which code in an application has been executed during testing or fuzzing.

☑ Statement coverage measures which lines or assembly instructions have been executed.

☑ Branch coverage indicates which conditionals have been taken.

☑ Path coverage examines which paths through the program have been run.

☑ Path coverage contains the most information, but due to the large number of paths, it is usually impossible to achieve a high percentage of path coverage.

Obtaining Code Coverage

☑ The *-fprofile-arcs* and *-ftest-coverage* gcc flags are required to produce code coverage.

☑ For cases when we don't have source code, the PaiMei framework may be used.

Improving Code Coverage with Fuzzing

☑ Code coverage can indicate locations in the application that require additional fuzzing.

☑ Additional test cases can be generated by hand by looking at untaken branches and tracing back to determine how the test cases should be modified.

☑ Improved test cases can be automatically generated by comparing the results of different test cases to the amount of code coverage they obtained. This is still experimental.

☑ Test cases may theoretically be generated by solving constraints on the user-supplied data to the program to yield maximal code coverage.

Weaknesses of Code Coverage

☑ Just because a line was *executed*, doesn't mean it was *fuzzed*.

☑ Only the attack surface can be reached, but code coverage does not take this into account.

Frequently Asked Questions

Q: I instrumented my program with gcov but it never produces any coverage information, what's the deal?

A: The coverage data is recorded in memory and is only dumped to the files on disk when the application exits. If the application runs indefinitely, like a server, or crashes, this never occurs. The easiest way to collect the data in such a situation is to attach to the process with a debugger, such as *gdb*, and force the application to exit (cleanly).

Q: Are there other tools are out there that can do code coverage?

A: Yes, there are many tools available. Some of the more popular ones include

- *Coverage Validator* from Software Verification. This requires the corresponding debug files.
- *Rational Purify/PureCoverage* from IBM. This requires the corresponding debug files.
- *Insure++* from Parasoft. This requires source code.
- *BullseyeCoverage* from Bullseye. This requires source code.
- *Vgprof*, an experimental Valgrind skin for Linux.

Q: Setting up my working environment to do code coverage can take a significant amount of time. Should I always worry about code coverage?

A: It never hurts to just trying fuzzing and see what happens. Code coverage is really best as a "tool of last resort." After you've fuzzed for a while with no luck and want to analyze exactly what is going on, it is time to look at code coverage. After all, the test cases you are sending might all have the wrong checksum and may all be getting rejected immediately!

Index

Printed and bound by CPI Group (UK) Ltd, Croydon, CR0 4YY

03/10/2024

01040340-0016